THE KILLJOY'S BOOK OF THE CINEMA

A SCHMOVIE GOER'S COMPANION

By John H. Irving
Illustrated by Kev Smith

Virgin

First published in Great Britain in 1985 by Virgin Books Ltd,
328 Kensal Road, London W10 5XJ

ISBN 0 86369 107 2

Printed and bound in Great Britain by Richard Clay Ltd
(The Chaucer Press), Suffolk

Typeset by Keyline Graphics, London NW6

Cover and design by Sue Walliker and Ursula Shaw

Distributed by Arrow Books

To BIFIWI
for fixing broken things

Kacknowledgements

I sometimes feel that gratitude can be overdone. One can only be so grateful to so many people in a book of this size before their names begin to read like the ingredients on a packet of muesli. For that reason, I intend to keep the thank-yous short, and consequently I am indebted to the following for their nominations and advice while the material was being compiled:–

To The Schmovie Club Bel Air Office: Glynis Morgan, Kelly MacCubbin;
New York Office: Alice Hecht, Jo Fahrenkopf;
Los Angeles Office: Sarah Clark;
New Mexico Office: Don Barron, Erin Barron;
Paris Office: Thierry Monod.

To my enthusiastic research assistant Angela Williams, who literally gave up minutes of her time to check and re-check the facts.

To Alex Bremer, Peter Dewhirst, Eva Glazer, Andrew Irving, David Jones, Peggy Keane, Justin Marsham, Tim Moat, Helen Norburn, James Pinder, Ian Pittaway, Catherine Pittaway, Mark Shaw, Kevin Smith, Bill Vousden, Brian Walters, Les Wilkins.

To Edward Agius at FCS, Annette Seymour Avedian at Videomedia, Alec at Elstree Studios, Derek Endean at Rank Video.

To John Brown and the team at Virgin for having the guts!

To Chris Riley and Mary Pett at the BBC, without whom *I* might not have had the guts!

And I think that's quite enough gratitude for one book, don't you?

Contents

The Cut That Wounds

The Cut That Wounds

Perfectionists are such pests, aren't they?

Yet there are times when the film industry seems riddled with them, worming their way into every corner, pressing for excellence, dismissing anything third-rate as inferior – until, in the end, far too much attention is given to those who are raising standards and getting things right, and not enough to the guy who tries hard, does the very best he can, and *still* cocks it up.

Sure, people are impressed by success, but equally they are fascinated by mistakes. They warm to humiliating failure and all the bloodletting and unpleasantness that go with it, in much the same way they crowd around serious road-accidents or a warehouse fire – open-mouthed, cringing, but all the while pushing for a better view. At such times, it is reassuring to know that the other man's ship has gone down, not yours; his plans and ambitions have capsized and sunk while your own are still tied safely to their moorings.

Schmovie-goers quite readily pander to this curiosity, by dusting off the greatest mistakes made in feature films over the past fifty years, and parading them before a public whose craving for kack is insatiable. You see, in our view, there is no shame in being slapdash, at least not when your efforts, by their very shoddiness, bring such pleasure to millions.

Excellence is fine in its place, but for sheer entertainment value, you can't beat a real botched job.

> *Captain Apache* (1971) The deputy sheriff is ambushed outside his office in the town of Paradise. He walks into the street, is attacked and shot twice, then falls back into the room, dead – but with a knife in his chest!

I am frequently asked the same old question: if I had to pinpoint a single magic ingredient, present in the making of any film, that almost certainly dooms it to flounder, what would it be? And I always give the same old answer: team-work. For no matter how slick and efficient the film-making process becomes, the quality of a production, and ultimately its success at the box-office, continue to hang on the strength of team-work behind it. Which is Good News for us, since it guarantees that every film set, well into the future, will have on it a chain of potential wreckers – actors, artists, craftsmen and technicians – all highly skilled, all highly fallible, and all working under intense pressure to bring their picture in on time and under budget; in fact, the ideal conditions for mistakes to flourish.

First in line to louse up a scene has got to be the man behind the camera. He has every chance to point it where he shouldn't: around the side of the set or into a large mirror, reflecting the crew and their equipment standing out of shot. However, if he fails us, and does his job properly, we still have high hopes that the chap with the microphone will swing it wildly across the top of the picture – not just licking the frame with it, that's no good – we want to see it drop down and hang in full view above the actor's head, as it does in *The Blob* (1958), or better still the man himself should appear in the film, waving the microphone frantically in the air, trying to pick up a difficult conversation, as in *The Last Voyage* (1960).

If the worst happens, however, and *he* gets it right, then not to worry! We just fall back on the continuity girl, and beyond her the lighting and special-effects people, the make-up artists, stuntmen, and so on down the chain. Add to these the scores of pitfalls lurking around hastily-built sets, bored animals, extras who can't act, children who don't want to, props that have a mind of their own, actresses that haven't, and you can see, there are a thousand avenues of imperfection clamouring to be explored. Goofs of unforgivable gravity are committed with astounding regularity. If you have not spotted any so far, it is only because you don't yet know where to look, or, more likely, you don't know precisely what it is you are looking for.

To the bewildered newcomer with the whole of motion picture history in front of him, there would seem to be an impossible range of opportunities for error, and no obvious signals within the films themselves to warn you that a mistake is on the way – although, having said that, every so often someone on the screen may unwittingly help you out.

> *Subterfuge* (1968) A high-ranking civil servant in his Whitehall office snaps at a colleague, 'Window!' It seems unimportant at first, but if you look more closely, you will see that the window behind him *has* changed shape. The large curved one he had a few seconds before has split into a couple of rectangular ones and moved further along the wall.

The only other example I can think of is:

> *Vera Cruz* (1953) in which Gary Cooper and Burt Lancaster play a pair of small-time opportunists escorting a carriage, a countess and a fortune in gold across Mexico in 1866. They are attacked by bandits en route, and during the fight Cooper shouts, 'The carriage, the carriage!' Sure enough, the bright red carriage has vanished from where they left it. It is only gone for a moment, mind you, and returns right afterwards, but had it not been for Gary Cooper you might not have seen it disappear at all.

That is the best you can hope for, I'm afraid, by way of help from the actors on screen. Most times, you are on your own. So unless you take the time to read this book, to learn the rules of schmovie-going and become a trained spotter, five or six real howlers may come and go and you'll miss the lot.

As President of the Schmovie Club, I frequently tour the provinces, addressing meetings, enlisting new members and delivering inspirational seminars. . .well, we call them seminars, but they are much more than that. I look on them as pep-talks for the down-at-heart – schmovie-buffs suffering from temporary kack-blindness, who haven't spotted a serious error in so long they have begun to wonder whether they ever will again.

'But how do we flush the little buggers out, John?' they plead so often. 'Where do we look?'

Straight away, I pull them into a darkened booth, and play them a brief clip from a chilling 1959 picture, *The World, the Flesh and the Devil,* which I carry about with me when necessary, to help refresh flagging spirits.

> North America is under threat from a cloud of radioactive dust. 'END OF THE WORLD' screams a newspaper headline. 'Millions flee from cities.' New York is deserted, except for Harry Belafonte and two others on board a small boat in the harbour. As the three of them chug slowly in to dock, Belafonte mutters despairingly, 'We are the total population of New York.' Though apparently not, because at this point a fourth, unidentified person comes into view, a man in white overalls on the wharf behind him. He strolls up to a workman's shed, opens the door and disappears inside.

Any doubters tend to perk up here, particularly when they learn how many other pictures contain exactly the same mistake. That little guy in white, whoever he is, is immensely important to us. Not just because he manages to spoil what is perhaps the most critical shot in the entire movie, but because he succeeds in doing exactly the same thing in dozens of other movies too. This man ruins films on a regular basis!

Now, you are probably saying to yourself, 'But I've never seen him before. I never *ever* spot mistakes in films.'

Of course you don't. But chances are that, so far, you have been doing all the wrong things. You'd be surprised how many people, when they visit the cinema, become totally immersed in the plot. Intent on following the story, they listen to the dialogue, absorb the twists and developments, wrap themselves in the special effects, and then leave, complaining that they didn't see any mistakes in it.

This is the Big Screen, remember? If you always look at what they want you to look at, you'll never see anything. Away from the centre of the picture and the main action lie acres of space, regularly teeming with little hiccups you were never intended to see. Naturally, I'm not suggesting you give the story a miss altogether. By all means keep half an ear on the dialogue, and be sure to glance every so often at what the actors are doing – you don't have to lose the thread completely. But at the same time, do poke about in the corners of the screen when you can. Ask yourself questions. Is the director standing in shot? Can you see the scaffolding holding the set up? Does that prehistoric woman have a zip in her costume?

Why, in *Mary Poppins* (1964), do Julie Andrew's gloves change from white to black to white again while she is reading a letter? Or how is it that impoverished artist Gene Kelly in *An American in Paris* (1951), can set out from home with eight paintings, sell two of them, and still return home with eight? Why, in *The Bible* (1966), does Adam, first man on Earth, created by God from dust, have a navel?

Above all, don't be afraid to look out of windows. You may be amazed at what you find.

> *The Bandwagon* (1953) is a classic film musical, directed by Vincente Minnelli. Fred Astaire and a company of actors, travelling by train to Baltimore, have taken over an entire carriage for the journey. It has eight windows in all, four down each side. The curious thing is that, outside two of them, it is daylight and the sun is shining, while out of the other six, it is night-time and cars are passing by with their head-lamps on.

'Impossible!' I hear you cry. 'They would take more care than that. They're professionals, for Chrissakes!'

This is good. A healthy scepticism on your part only spices up the challenge on mine. All I can say to you now is that by the time your schmovie training is complete, I promise that you will accept such things not as exceptional, but as very much the norm. Trust me.

A couple of points before we go on: first, never be put off by the term 'classic film', or by the status and prestige of the people behind it. Directors of impeccable pedigree make mistakes like anyone else.

> *Ryan's Daughter* (1970) A blue army jacket with a red collar is hung up on the back of a door and left there. In most circumstances, you would forget about something like that, but if you stick with it and keep watching, you will see that, seconds later, the collar suddenly turns from red to blue. And this from David Lean, whose reputation as a stickler for detail is legend. However, before you become too smug, it is one of the very few occasions when you will find something going awry in a David Lean picture. The man is so pernickety.

As a newcomer to schmovie-going, if it bothers you to tangle with the likes of Lean or Minnelli first off, or with Alfred Hitchcock, John Ford, Stanley Kubrick, or any of the other all-time greats, my advice is to paddle in the shallows for a while. If you can't bear to pick holes in Steven Spielberg's latest, for instance, go back to one of his earlier efforts – *Duel* (1971) maybe, or *Sugarland Express* (1974) – and try your hand at those. Start humble and cheap at the beginning and work up. That way, you will lose your inhibitions gently, in stages, and collect a personal repertoire of goofs as you go. Very soon, you will have all the confidence you need to fault their later work.

The second point is this: don't, whatever you do, be fooled by high standards. The dividing line between brilliance and bunkum is sometimes a slim one. All may look wonderful on the surface, but underneath, behind that glossy veneer of professionalism, everything favours disarray. Films are not filmed in the correct order for a start. Shots are shot higgledy-piggledy and spliced together later, with patience, love, know-how and an enormous amount of care – though at times you honestly doubt it.

> *Thunderball* (1965) James Bond (Sean Connery) and CIA agent Felix Leiter fly out to sea in a helicopter to locate a sunken ship. At the point where Bond is preparing to make his first dive, Leiter is wearing

> trousers from one angle, but from the other he's got shorts on.

Scenes that appear consecutively in the finished film like this, may have been shot months and miles apart. Locations are frequently on different continents, and only when the hundreds of pieces of film are assembled by the editor and laid end to end in the proper order do many of the discrepancies come to light, by which time it is usually too late anyway: filming has wrapped, sets have been torn down, actors have drifted off to work elsewhere and, likely as not, cash is running low, too.

Of course, the continuity bods do what they can. Using extensive on-the-spot notes and photographs while filming is in progress, they try to ensure that the leading actor does not enter a lift in T-shirt and jeans, and leave it wearing a tweed suit. But such is the infinite complexity involved in making movies, that they really haven't a hope of matching all the shots up completely. There are bound to be gaps occasionally, and they know it.

> *Carry on Behind* (1975) Ian Lavender walks up to the shower-block on a campsite, with a yellow bath-towel over his right shoulder. He opens the door and steps inside, and now the towel is a red floral one slung over his left shoulder.

On these occasions, the editor is powerless to help, having been presented with a *faute accomplie*. No amount of fancy editing by him will smooth out the differences between the two shots – in fact, he may as well knot the ends together, for all the good it would do. In which case, if they can't afford to reshoot and they can't afford to cut the scene out, then the only choice they have is no choice. They must join up the pieces regardless, and pray to God nobody will notice, which is more Good News for us because, luckily, God has no time for film-makers – some say he is still punishing them for what they did to the Ten Commandments. And as a result, mistakes in films are more abundant than ever, while the number of people out to spot them increases daily, making schmovie-going the fastest-growing blood sport in this country today.

The appeal lies, I'm sure, in its simplicity. Anyone can have a go. All it takes is a bit of patience and a keen sense of timing. To be able to know beforehand what will go wrong with a film and when, is a talent I can only liken to a sixth sense. Some folks have it naturally, but the rest of us need to work at it until we can spot mistakes without too much effort. You have got to be willing to wait. Give a film time to go wrong, be patient and you should be amply rewarded.

Some mistakes happen in the blink of an eye, and these we call flash-flaws. They tend to be the smaller kind of continuity errors – petty, niggling things, not important in themselves, but just obvious enough to catch the eye, such as the cigarette that leaps from Sean Connery's lips into the ashtray by his side, completely of its own accord, in *Dr No* (1962); or the pendant hanging around a woman's neck one moment and dangling loosely over her hand the next in *Raiders of the Lost Ark* (1981); or the ring that mysteriously disappears from Yul Brynner's ear while he is singing 'It's a puzzlement' in *The King and I* (1956).

Flash-flaws are everywhere. They have a quaint now-you-see-it-now-you-don't quality, which means, therefore, that you must be quick to nab them.

Pal Joey (1957) An angry chorus-girl in a night-club canteen throws a stick of celery down on to the table, but storms out of the room with it still in her hand.

Where the Spies Are (1965) John Le Mesurier takes a cigar out of his pocket and smokes it without lighting it first.

The Shining (1981) Jack Nicholson attacks his bathroom door with a logging axe, and chops through the right-hand panel. He doesn't touch it again after that, but the very next minute, *both* sides of the door have been chopped out.

Family Plot (1976) Bruce Dern is seated at the kitchen table, about to eat a hamburger. He unscrews the top from a ketchup bottle, pauses for a moment, then picks up the same bottle again and unscrews the top a second time. After pouring ketchup on his burger, he screws the lid on the bottle and puts it down on the table. Almost immediately, the top is back off and lying at his side.

Other mistakes, called 'middle-rangers', take a while longer:

Eraserhead (1976) Henry Spencer, the main character, steps in a puddle with his right foot as he walks back to his bedsit. Unfortunately, you then have to follow him all the way home before you can watch him take his *left* sock off and hang that over the radiator to dry.

> *Custer of the West* (1968) The Cheyenne Indians tie two rogue goldminers to a cart and push them down a steep road. At the top of the hill, as they start rolling, one of the men is wearing a white hat, the other a black one. But at the bottom, when the cart topples over a cliff, both of their hats are white.

We refer to this as the 'Knock on Wood' Effect, chiefly because that is what it's called, but also because it originated in a film of the same name – which, alas, starred Danny Kaye, so we try not to refer to it very much at all.

> *Knock on Wood* (1954) One evening, while staying at a London hotel, Kaye finds a dead body skewered to his wardrobe door. The alarm is raised and someone calls the police. Downstairs, a young constable darts into the lobby wearing a pointed helmet, but by the time he reaches Kaye's bedroom, a matter of seconds later, he's wearing a peaked cap.

An extremely poor film on all counts, and one of Danny Kaye's best. Although, in fairness to him, I should say that when I saw it I was still convalescing after seeing his previous one, so maybe I was a little unreceptive. What this picture did, however, was to prove once and for all something schmovie-goers had suspected for a long time – that hats in a film mean big trouble.

> *Earth Versus the Flying Saucers* (1956) A cycle cop, parked at the roadside wearing a crash helmet and a light shirt, moves out on to the highway in a dark uniform and peaked cap.

> *Assault on Precinct 13* (1976) Two more cops, this time in a patrol car, swing into the forecourt of a deserted police station. From a distance they have caps on; close up, they haven't.

> *633 Squadron* (1964) During a surprise bombing raid on a British airfield, Cliff Robertson dives for cover behind a bunker. From the back he is wearing a cap, from the front it's gone.

> *The Blue Max* (1966) Derren Nesbitt, sitting in the back of a German troop-wagon, takes his hat off twice without putting it on in between.

Trouble In Store (1953) Margaret Rutherford tries on a fashionable hat with two feathers glued to the brim. First she is wearing it the right way round and then, in the next shot, back to front.

Tom Thumb (1958) Woody, the happy-go-lucky woodcutter, has two red feathers in his cap. . .sometimes. Other times, he has an extra brown one which just comes and goes as it pleases.

Finally, at the extreme, you have a smaller number of long-haul mistakes, those that seem to dawdle for an absolute age before finally going wrong. You'll find it a real test of your stamina and determination to follow them through until they do.

The Wild Bunch (1969) Somewhere in the middle of the film, the oldest member of the gang, Freddie Sykes, is shot in the right thigh by a sniper. In great pain, he retires from the story. When he returns, almost at the end, he is wearing a grubby, blood-stained bandage – around his *left* thigh.

I believe that the longest anyone has ever waited to check out a mistake is between one film and its sequel.

By the end of *Jaws* (1975), most of the fishing-boat ORCA has been eaten away by the shark. What it doesn't eat, sinks. Pay attention, as the boat goes down, to the serial number painted on the bow – MS 15 LF – because at the beginning of *Jaws 2* (1978), when the wreck is being inspected by divers on the seabed, there is no serial number. Instead, it now has a shiny new brass nameplate with the word ORCA spelled out on it.

An experienced director knows that the best place in his film for a flaw to be slipped in, if he has one, is right at the start, and preferably before the opening titles if possible. Any mistake, however catastrophic, can be tucked away there in the confidence that it will probably go unnoticed. Which is why so many of the older horror pictures used to open with a quick scene-setting shot of a distant mountain-range that was obviously fake and painted on glass: crayoned alps with a thoroughly unconvincing water-colour monastery perched on top, or an abbey that had bright blue walls and a scarlet roof; roughly-sketched two-dimensional prisons, castles, convents, forts, any place they couldn't afford to build in the studio for themselves or travel far afield to film.

The logic behind this ploy is simple. By showing you their cheapest, most inept shot in the first minute, there is every chance that when it comes up on the screen, you will still be settling down in your seat, scratching the cellophane off your Poppets, or smoothing the creases out of your Pacamac and folding it away. The mistake is slipped in so furtively, and so early on, that it catches you off-guard. An infuriating piece of skullduggery! Only seconds into the picture and you've missed the most important part.

> *The Black Knight* (1954) Barely have the house-lights dimmed on this one, when a jolly minstrel rides into view, plucking a lute and belting out a punchy medieval ballad about boldness and spunk. All of a sudden, the colour of his tights changes from red to blue – even before the Columbia Pictures logo has flashed on to the screen.

If the mistake won't fit in at the beginning, but nevertheless needs to be buried somewhere where it might not be seen, then the next best place is at the very end. The audience never expects anything untoward so late in the story. Most of them by that time are bending down to scoop up their things, and looking around for the closest exit – making it the perfect place to slip in a quick one. Or, even better, if the picture is especially dreary, there's every chance they may either have dozed off, or become so hugely fed up with waiting for it to end, that they've packed up and gone home.

It's all a matter of psychology.

> *Attila the Hun* (1954) On a weary trek across Italy with his army, in the closing minutes of an even wearier film, Attila lapses into a fever. His men want him to set down and rest, but no: 'On to Rome!' he cries, and gallops away on his giant white stallion. A few hundred yards further on, around the next hill, Attila runs across the Pope, sitting on *his* white horse in the middle of a river. And since it would not do for the Force of Good and the Force of Evil both to have white horses, by the time Attila reaches the river himself, he is riding a black one.

Hang on, though: before you go jumping to the wrong conclusion, I ought to say that, as the audience, we have no way of knowing whether, in the *Black Knight*, *Jaws* and *Attila* examples, the mistakes were planted by accident or design. And I might also add that we don't much care either. All that matters to us is that they are there, on full display every time those movies are shown.

Wherever it happens to be, and no matter how long it takes to appear, the dedicated enschmoviast will chase after a goof and winkle it out with an almost evangelical zeal. And it is this total commitment on the part of Club members that so infuriates the film industry. Each time we nail a new release, we hear yet another outcry from our critics. 'Killjoys', they call us, 'Nit-pickers', 'Armchair know-alls', criticizing things not one of us could do better ourselves. They may have a point, I suppose. There is a lot of truth in the allegation that when schmovie buffs visit the cinema, they are not so much watching the film as picketing the screen. But what the moaners don't seem to realize is that schmovie-going has quite a history behind it. It's not a new phenomenon by any means.

Much of what we recognize as the sport of kack-spotting nowadays began as an unfortunate by-product of the industry's own greed and cunning as far back as the early 1950s, when British cinema chains were running a heavy recruitment drive to attract children with special matinee performances on Saturday mornings. These were intended to lure tomorrow's adults into picture-houses, to get them hooked early and sold on the idea of being regular patrons in the future, a policy thrust upon individual theatre managements and their staff who, in many cases, were far from sold on the idea themselves, fearing the wilder yob element that seemed to surface in even the gentlest, most harmless 10-year-old child when let loose without his parents in a public place. The odds at these shows could be quite horrifying: one nervous ice-cream lady in pinny and cap, with a tray of drinks-on-sticks and an uncertain smile, against two hundred shouting, stomping, marauding hooligans.

Schmovie-going really evolved out of the Saturday morning matinees and the films they showed, in particular those wretched cliffhanger serials imported from the States. Every week a fresh episode identical to the previous one. Twenty thrilling minutes of mystery, double-cross, breathless pursuit and running fist-fights, terminating in some impossible peril from which the hero would always deftly escape next time, not because he was special in any way, or because of his 'powers', but because the writer had usually changed the plot so drastically to save him.

Whether he was strapped into the path of a circular saw, tied up in the back of a truck as it skidded down a ravine and burst into flames, or slumped unconscious at the joystick of a toy plane hurtling out of control on strings against a painted sky – at the last moment, he would always be written out of danger by the skin of his teeth. Whole sets would have to be rearranged to provide a sudden get-out, an escape route that was not there, you'd swear it, the previous week. 'Quick,

Mary, down this airshaft!', or 'Oh look! Here's an abandoned row-boat – come on, let's go!', or 'If. . .I could. . .just reach that. . .bunch of keys. . .' *That bunch of keys* would be at least 20 feet away at the end of Chapter 7. But by the start of Chapter 8, it was almost at arm's length. After some frantic wriggling across the floor, with the fuse crackling swiftly down to the explosives, he would unlock his chains, untie his fiancée from the acid vat and shout, 'Quick! Behind these rocks!' The very rocks that would protect them from the blast and the acid, and which were also not there the week before.

All outrageously far-fetched, of course, and a feast for the easily-pleased, but at the same time popular and very successful. Republic Pictures alone produced 66 serials between 1936 and 1955, with titles so provocative they defied you not to go and see them: *Panther Girl of the Kongo, Zorro's Black Whip, G-Men Never Forget, King of the Rocketmen.* All done on chicken-feed budgets, each episode seemingly cheaper than the last, although once you had seen episode 1 it was often hard to imagine how the rest *could* get any cheaper. We used to sit there week after week, trying to spot the point where the money ran out.

The stories rarely strayed from a standard three-tier formula:

1. Good fighting Evil.
2. The hero's girlfriend being tied to a sofa.
3. Good triumphing over Evil.

At that time, it was very much the woman's lot to spend long periods gagged and roped to a chair or post, with the additional duties of looking pretty, fainting to form a diversion, then becoming hysterical and having to be slapped. It was the girl's job in a chase to trip, fall and be captured; in a crisis to scream, trip, fall and be captured; and in a tight corner to panic, scream, trip, fall and be captured, after which she had no further responsibility but to stand and wait until the hero could bound to her side, adjusting his suit, lifting a slick of hair back across his ear, and say, 'Are you okay, Mary?' As grisly and hackneyed as it sounds now, this love-interest/helpless-maiden tag set a role for women in the cinema that lasted another 20 years, and which they are still finding hard to shake off.

All the best heroes wore silly costumes with an emblem on the chest and stood for justice, wholesome values, road safety and clean underwear. Many of them also had tiny eye-masks that somehow prevented even their family and best friends recognizing who they were. The best villains, by contrast, were master-criminals whose true identity was concealed beneath a hooded robe. All had sinister and venomous names – The Viper, The Scorpion, Ming the Merciless, The White Spirit, The Five O'Clock Shadow, The Gnat – together with a corresponding 'shape' (viper-shape, scorpion shape, etc.) sewn lovingly on to the back of their outfit by their mother. The villain never seemed to run short of henchmen; he had an army of them, in baggy trousers with large turn-ups, trilby hats that stayed on their head during a brawl, and a jacket two sizes too large. The henchies were willing to fight for their master and protect him from attack, without any apparent justification for doing so, and with the sole reward of receiving a regular beating twice each episode, and perhaps the chance of being killed. Yet the reserves never ran low. Once the old lot were too crippled to carry on, they were pensioned off and a new batch brought in.

The cast-lists for the serials were made up largely of anonymous actors. A galaxy of unknowns played in these B-pictures, delivering awkward jerky performances as though their obscurity depended on it. And each line they uttered, each anguished pause, faltering step and exaggerated amateurish gesture was greeted by jubilant yelps of derision from the front stalls. Undecided whether to cheer the hero or hiss the villain, we did neither and settled for booing the whole film.

Simple and undemanding as they were, however, they transformed the innocent ritual of going to the cinema on a Saturday morning into a crucial part of the weekly routine for thousands of youngsters up and down the country, who were drawn by the foolproof blend of feature films, top-of-the-voice singalongs, yo-yo competitions and indiscriminate violence that were the hallmarks of these two-hour shows.

The audience could be broken down into three distinct factions. At the front, in the first two rows, were the Ovalteenies – meek, moot, agog – together with the nancy-boys in their Ribena-stained duffle-coats, one or two State orphans on day-release, and a smuggle of immigrants, plus the usual debris of vagabonds and winos left over from Friday evening's performance. They made it their practice to slip into the lavatories during 'God Save the Queen', not to emerge again before first light. That way they got a warm cubicle for the night, all the Jeyes fluid they could drink, and the guarantee of a film-show and jolly sing-song when they woke up next morning.

Right at the back sat the Nicoteenies: delinquent smokers, annexed by their guilt as they puffed arrogantly on their father's dimps, playing with a habit that would one day kill 13.7% of them. Uncontrollable, they were – cracking their knuckles to a popular rhythm, running Longest-Nadger contests in the far gangway, and carving their initials into the usherettes, as their way of impressing the third faction, the girls, who were far too preoccupied anyway, nursing long-held dreams of sitting on Pinocchio's face while he told them an endless stream of lies. So much puberty all in one place!

And then there was us. Not a faction at all really – we went to see the films, and were the kind of model children the cinema chains were hoping to net in their recruitment drive. We centred ourselves on the fifth row in the stalls, and on one seat especially – E23: five rows back and midway between the aisles. A little close, perhaps, but it offered an uncompromising view of the screen. From E23 there were no mysteries. Even the most expensive effects became hopelessly transparent at that distance. We could see that the men Captain Marvel was throwing against rocks were just floppy, straw-filled bags; that the rocks themselves were simply polystyrene painted grey. We knew that the only reason the hero could fly at all was because he was suspended from a gantry on two lengths of piano-wire. We began looking for traces of the camera crew standing in shot, shadows of the microphone cast across the sky, special effects that weren't special at all – such as the flimsy scale-model helicopter that wavered and tilted in the draught from the wind-machine.

It was plain to us even at that age that producers had been raping the archives for any spare footage they might use to link the parts of the story they could afford to shoot with other parts which they couldn't. They took filler shots from other films – fights, car-crashes, chases – and spliced them into their own, to make one irregular jarring whole, jammed full of excitement, and full of continuity mistakes as well. It was quite regular for one shot not to tie up with its neighbour.

> *King of the Rocketmen* (1949) A lorry careers off the end of a jetty, losing two of its wheels as it falls, but has them back in place by the time it hits the water.
>
> Two motorcycle cops screech out of a layby in white helmets, but turn the next bend wearing peaked caps. (This later became the 'Knock on Wood' Effect.)

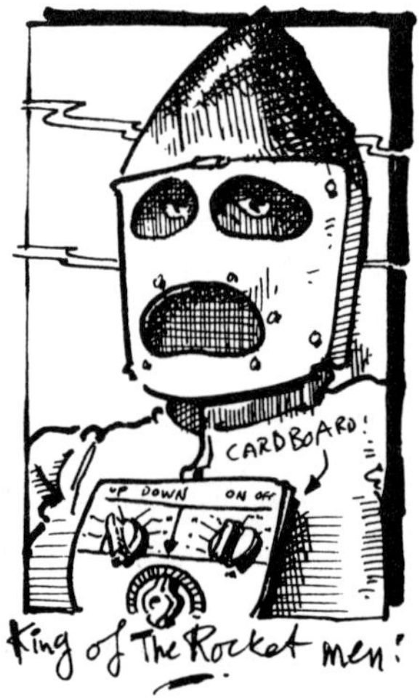

Every mistake ever conceived appeared in these films at least once – twice if there was time, and as more and more of them were shown to younger and younger audiences, a new breed of juvenile intolerant emerged, one with a built-in resistance to razzmatazz, hardened against the magic that had so captivated the generation before us. By the time we turned 14, we were no longer dazzled by the bright lights, and what began as silly childish cynicism later crystallized into a broad resistance and then into active defiance, before finally it became what we now recognize as the make-up of the disciplined, dedicated schmovie-goer, who still feels committed to cinema, but treasures a mild contempt borne of over-familiarity with the workings of the industry.

From that point, the quest for kack was on!

The Schmovie Club was set up in 1983 as both a refuge for flaw-fanatics and a central body to catalogue fresh mistakes, also as a tribunal to arbitrate in any disputes. Schmovie-goers are a damned argumentative bunch. Members crawl over each other's backs to reach a mistake first. You'll see them on the opening night of a film's release, maybe even at the premiere, down in the fifth row as always, pointing wildly at the screen, haggling over awkward details, then scribbling down their finds. That first night is crucial to them; they feel they must be present at the birth, so to speak. Indeed, one group we know of in the North of England, calling themselves The Friends of Herod, make special efforts to attend early press showings of films to ensure that they reach the mistakes in them before anyone else does.

This is by no means exceptional either. All over the country breakaway groups such as this have formed, out of our control but each of them sharing a common goal – to root out kack wherever it may lie. And that is not all they have in common. First, they have all given themselves splendidly enigmatic names, such as The Bonus Breed, The Squealers, Wait-Watchers, Sneakthief Squaddies 6-66 and The Purley Queens. Second, all of their members show a profound interest in heavy drinking, and regularly try to pass off their illicit pub crawls as 'discussion socials'. And third, many seem to suffer from an uncomfortable complaint known as The Schmovie Thumb, a strain produced by fast-forwarding or rewinding a video recorder for long periods while scanning a film for goofs.

Unfortunately, as with many growing organizations, The Schmovie Club has been infiltrated of late by one or two obsessive individuals, members so out of check with current thinking they even watch Danny Kaye films for pleasure, a stand I personally find bizarre, almost other-worldly. Elsewhere, a few less-extremists sit through *The Poseidon Adventure* time and again, just waiting for the part where Shelley Winters drowns. Plus, as you might expect, we have our unfair share of 'Oh, and did you see the bit where. . .?' bores, who tend to knock back one too many Babychams at parties, then corner you in the kitchenette and rattle off 300 of their latest, *very favourite* mistakes, one after the other, without pausing to see if you are listening. Schmovie intellectuals are as welcome as lepers on the social circuit, and talking to one can be awfully oppressive – a bit like being kissed by a choir.

We set no limits officially to the kind of films we cover. The field is wide open. No picture will be excluded because the reviews were rotten, or the budget too low, or because it grossed too much at the box-office. In theory, everything is fair game. However, unofficially, and in practice, to keep things under control, we do draw the line at certain points.

Most of the films we vet were released after 1940. That way we are allowing the cinema a sort of childhood, a head-start and a chance to grow to an acceptable standard, before we start to kick and bully it. People often look to us in the hope of finding some of the top stars from the silent era in our files. But the likes of Charlie Chaplin, Buster Keaton and Fatty Arbuckle were around too early for us. Fatty Arbuckle has never been considered a schmovie-star; therefore, except for these two sentences and the next one, he is not mentioned in this book again. From now on, consider this book a Fatty Arbuckle-Free Zone.

Also shortlisted for exclusion are Ken Russell films – much too gross; anything by Michael Winner; animated pictures, on the grounds that cartoons generally are a triumph of fantasy over fallibility, and as such wriggle through the net. Besides, in order to check a Walt Disney full-length animated feature, one has to wade through such a quagmire of niceness – all that goody-goody whistling, shaking hands with chimney-sweeps and kissing deer. . .Pah! No, cartoons are definitely out; as are TV movies and, lastly, sex films. They are far too tawdry and cut-price even for us, and tend to be the domain mostly of crumpled divorcees in sticky-stained gaberdines and PVC weeding gloves.

With sex films, the plots are virtually non-existent, following the same kind of format each time: two Finnish hair-stylists, Olga and Giupetta, rent a chalet for a snorkling holiday on the shores of the Skagerrak. Olga takes off into town with a great Dane she had sex with on the coach coming down. Giupetta is looking forward to a quiet night in, and has just started smearing Marmite across her breasts when the doorbell rings. It's Øsvenson, a freelance linoleum layer from Trondheim, whom she and Olga both had sex with in the coach station before they came down. First he lays her linoleum, and then her, after which it's pretty much unabridged knøbbing right up until the closing credits. They break off once usually, for her to comb her hair and for him to twist the ring-pull off a Holsten, but these few seconds respite provide the only let-up in their otherwise humdrum sexual routine.

For no reason other than that, films such as *Sex at 7000 Feet, Cop-Caners of Hong Kong, Crazy Bonkers, A Big Tip for the Little Waitress,* and *Girl Guides Get It on Venus* are, to my relief if nobody else's, OUT!

If this is your first brush with schmovie-going, my advice is to treat it rather like a safari into the wild. You'll find the terrain uneven, and it's uphill most of the way. So break up your expedition once in a while to pitch camp and rest. Above all, be warned! – the natives in this area can be quite unpleasant. It's an untypical director who will clap you about the shoulders and thank you sincerely for faulting his work. We're pricking egos here. Pride is involved, and maybe a little perfectionism, too, so think on. It may have taken two years or longer to bring the film to the screen; millions of dollars will surely have been poured into the production; the solid graft of scores of performers, technicians and artists have gone into its making. They are trying to entertain *you* remember!

Because of the importance film-makers attach to their own work, we call shots that contain goofs of any sort 'mis-takes', rather than labelling the goofs themselves as 'errors'. Errors suggest incompetence, which is usually not the case at all.

Finally, try and be generous where you can. There are thousands of mis-takes around. You don't have to nit-pick to collect a repertoire. Let a few of the smaller slips go as dramatic licence.

> *Thoroughly Modern Millie* (1967) Mary Tyler Moore presses the twelfth-floor button in a hotel elevator, and gets out when it stops – on the tenth.
>
> *The Exorcist* (1973) Ellen Burstyn lights a cigarette, takes a couple of puffs and throws it away. Next minute it is back in her hand again.
>
> *National Lampoon's Animal House* (1978) Donald Sutherland chalks up the word 'SATAN' on a blackboard, with the letter T to the right-hand side of a crack in the board. As he speaks afterwards, the T jumps to the left-hand side of the crack.
>
> *Xanadu* (1980) The hall in which Gene Kelly hopes to open a roller-disco club has the word 'AUDITORIUM' spelled above the door, but with the letters A, T and R missing – except at night, when the T is back in place.
>
> *Trouble in Store* (1953) Margaret Rutherford glues three stickers to a suitcase, and walks away with four on it.

The people who make films succeed on their own terms, but they fail on ours. Go to your task with humour and humility and *please*, be kind!

Now, having said that. . .

Misplacing The

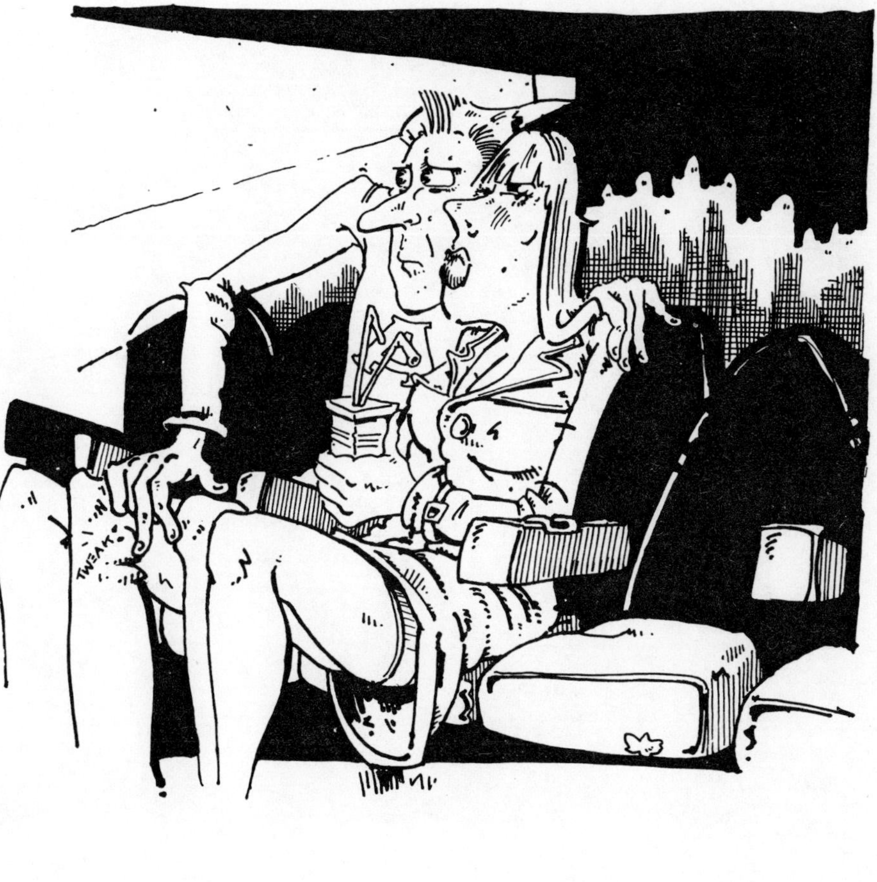

Misplacing The

BING-BONG!!
Will-ill Doctor-ctor Brewster-ster please-ss contact-act reception-shun! Doctor-ctor Brewster-ster t-to reception-shun. . .

On the whole, relations between members of the Schmovie Club are fairly good. The atmosphere at meetings is tense, but apart from the odd bust-up and one or two isolated quarrels, everyone seems to get on like Michael Jackson on fire. However, there is one subject that can always be relied upon to raise a few hackles, and that's jargon.

It was inevitable that as the popularity of schmovie-going grew, so too would the amount of jargon surrounding it: in-house words and phrases such as BLAAAAA!-men, reactioneers, 'dunwanna' rainfall and readily-deadlies, all meaningless outside the sport, but which can sometimes be hopelessly baffling to members and newcomers alike. One specific term seems to cause no end of confusion, and therefore deserves a sub-heading all to itself.

Utility Objects

> *Grease* (1979) John Travolta and a few friends set about converting a rusty clapped-out jalopy into a sleek high-speed racing machine. But the car is so broken-down and corroded that the job could take days. Out of desperation, they do what people in films generally do when they have an impossible task to complete in a few short hours – they sing and dance about it!

Film-makers discovered long ago that even the dullest, most odious chores can be completed in a fraction of the normal time simply by setting them to music. In the space of three verses, four choruses and a reprise, whole platoons of men can be assembled and trained for action, forts constructed from scratch, run-down hotels cleaned up and opened for business, railroads laid, bedrooms tidied, Rome built in a day, and useless heaps of metal customized into gleaming hot-rods. No doubt about it – choreography gets things done!

> So Travolta wastes no time: he leaps on to a work-bench and squeals, 'This car could be systematic. . .Hydromatic. . .' He peels off his leather jacket. 'Ultramatic. . .' He spins the jacket round above his head and flings it on to the shelf behind him. 'Why, it could be greased lightnin'. . .' And away he goes into the song. And away also goes the jacket off the shelf. As fast as that, it's gone.

And what is more, we knew it would, because it is what we call a utility jacket. Before I explain why, let me give you another example.

> *Silk Stockings* (1957) Cyd Charisse walks into her suite at a Paris hotel, lays down her typewriter on the table next to a vase of flowers and starts to pound away at it. In strides Fred Astaire and escorts her on to the verandah to squint at the view. By now, as a trainee schmovie-buff, you should know better than to be gazing idly across the rooftops. The first chance you get, look beyond the couple on the balcony and back into the room. You'll see that both the typewriter and the flowers have gone from the table – vanishing the moment they were no longer needed.

The utility object in a scene is anything – a prop, a person, perhaps even a building or landscape – that stays in view for the exact length of time it needs to be there, and then right afterwards completely disappears. In *Fancy Pants* (1950) it was an apron slung carelessly over a banister-rail by Bob Hope as he goes to answer the front door, while in *Marnie* (1964) it was two drinking glasses left by Sean Connery and Tippi Hedren on a table at the Atlantic City racecourse. Just as easily it could be a handkerchief, a shovel, a brooch or the magazine a man tucks into his overcoat pocket – in this case, the magazine itself could vanish, or the overcoat, even the man wearing the overcoat may go. You never can tell.

Whatever it turns out to be, the test is always the same: had it outlived its usefulness by the time it disappeared? If so, then that is your utility object. If not, and it was still in use, all you have is a simple continuity mis-take.

> *Chapter Two* (1979) Joe Bologna goes to such trouble to fasten the collar of his shirt and put on his tie, only to find that by the time he is ready to go out, the tie has disappeared and his collar is wide open.

Mausoleum (1983) A woman is dressing ready for a visit to her doctor. She puts on a jacket, pulls it down and adjusts it. Then she turns to face her husband and – ta-raaaa! – she is just wearing a blouse again – no jacket.

The ta-raaaa! is mine, incidentally. The overall effect of spotting mis-takes is diminished only by there being no fanfare to accompany them as they appear on the screen, so, I'm afraid, you have to put in your own.

Bologna's tie and the jacket both left while they were still in use, making them plain old continuity mis-takes. Utility objects take their leave only after they have been thrown aside and forgotten – out of mind, out of sight, you might say. However, don't be too eager to put things down to oversight. There may be times when what you think is a mis-take is merely a crafty way for the director to clear the decks and rid the screen of useless clutter ready for the next scene.

The Belle of New York (1952) Fred Astaire and a dozen young ladies, all of them beautiful, but in a 1950s-musical-kind-of-a-way, are dining at a long table stacked high with food, cutlery and crockery, plus a vase of flowers and a champagne bucket. The focus of attention shifts away from the meal – for a few seconds, no more. By the time we return, someone has cleared the table. Everything has been taken away except for the table-cloth and the flowers. The reason? Fred Astaire has to shimmy and cavort across it as part of the next dance number, and how could he, with all that half-eaten food lying around?

Some objects, temporarily forgotten, will disappear only to return again later on, when people are prepared to take more notice of them.

Showboat (1951) After the opening number, a grinning black woman in a red dress is standing on the staircase of the *Steamship Cotton Blossom* – but only very occasionally, in alternate shots. Otherwise she's gone.

King of the Rocketmen (1949) Rocketman's girlfriend, Glenda Thomas, has been tied to a sofa in her apartment whilst a violent knockabout punch-up crashes around behind her. All attention is focused on the fight and none on her, so she leaves. For a short while, there's nobody on the sofa, although she does return in time for the fight to finish and to be rescued.

Recently, real confusion has arisen over the number of things people are including under this heading. Mis-takes that can't be slotted neatly into a pigeon-hole elsewhere tend to be lumped together and called 'utility', regardless of the true definition of the word. Here are just a few examples, and you can judge for yourself.

Diamonds Are Forever (1971) Sean Connery, as James Bond, steals a four-wheeled Moon-buggy from a scientific research centre. As it swerves past the camera, the rough, rocky terrain proves too much for it, and it loses one of its wheels which, rather embarrassingly, bounces back into shot across the bottom corner of the screen. Now, very probably, that was the end of filming for the day. The buggy must have come to a shuddering halt off-camera and had to be repaired before they could carry on. Yet, in the very next shot in the film, the buggy is undamaged with its wheel back in place, and it rattles off into the distance.

Firestarter (1984) Two US Government agents pull into the side of the road with a flat tyre. While they jack up the car, the truck they are chasing passes by along the highway. Furious, one shouts to the other, 'Did you get the number?' 'Yeh, I got it,' comes the reply, as he jots something down in his notebook, though I can't think what, because the truck doesn't have a number. There is no licence-plate on the front or the back.

1984 (1984) Richard Burton snaps out one of John Hurt's front teeth as part of his torture. But seconds later, in Room 101, Hurt has a full set of teeth again.

Double Bunk (1960) A sailor in white shirt-sleeves bends over to reach for a sandwich. When he sits up straight, he has a blue jacket on.

Duel (1971) After being chased downhill at 90mph by a malicious diesel-truck driver, Dennis Weaver calls in at a roadside bar-grill for a breather. The waitress brings him a glass of water, which he drains. He puts the glass down on the table, and suddenly it is full of water again.

Fire Maidens From Outer Space (1956) A team of astronauts led by Sidney Tafler lands on one of Jupiter's moons. Tafler checks the time. The camera moves in and we are shown a close-up of his watch against the frayed cuff of his sleeve, which is strange because he's wearing a T-shirt.

The oddest category of the lot is perhaps the utility stiff. You'd think that anyone would be hard-pressed to bungle death, but it does happen in rare cases; a character achieves some sort of temporary passing away before being resurrected almost immediately.

Two Flags West (1950) A fierce battle during the American Civil War has resulted in many Indians being killed, including the one we are interested in, who is lying where he fell in the gateway to Fort Worth. Although, if you look again, you can see that he is just squatting, not dead at all. Even his horse is pretending. Just as everything is going well for our two little crouching casualties, an unexpected turn of events causes the Indian to panic. A column of Confederate troops heads for the fort, galloping towards the gate where the Indian is crouching, which means that if he stays where he is, he will be trampled to death, but for real this time. So, thinking quickly, and though dead, he pulls up his horse and hobbles stealthily out of the way behind a wall to let the soldiers through.

> *Apache* (1954) Burt Lancaster's horse collapses with exhaustion while he is riding it, so he pulls it to one side and shoots it. But when you see him the very next day, he is riding it again.

And my own personal favourite:

> *Royal Flash* (1975) Two men struggling on a bridge eventually overbalance and topple into the water below. As they fall, one of them loses his head – it comes right off and bounces away downstream. In any circumstances, this would be regarded as a misfortune. Here, it's a disaster, because the man whose head it is, a character called De Gautet, appears in the film for several minutes afterwards, and it is quite a surprise to see him pull himself out of the river a moment later and sit on a large rock rubbing his neck.

A variety of different items have been given the thin-air treatment over the years. These are the real utility objects, and I should mention some of the more well-known ones, enough to illustrate the idea, leaving you to go out and find the rest for yourself.

To start you off, you'll find a utility telephone-box in *The Young Ones* (1961), a utility text-book in *Tiara Tahiti* (1962), a utility shopping-bag in *Genevieve* (1954), a utility globe in *Carry on Spying* (1964), a utility sword in *Knights of the Round Table* (1953), a utility beer-bottle in *Let the People Sing* (1942), a utility futuristic New York skyline in *Death Race 2000* (1975), a utility ice-cream spoon in *Bugsy Malone* (1976), a utility bar-tender in *Escape From Fort Bravo* (1953), utility arrows in *Stagecoach* (1939), another utility jacket in *Ryan's Daughter* (1970), utility broken car headlamps in *For Your Eyes Only* (1981), a utility wound in *Last Feelings* (1980), utility blood off the blade of a knife in *Hound of the Baskervilles* (1959), and a utility dangerous hole in a rickety rope bridge in *Indiana Jones and the Temple of Doom* (1984).

Because it is becoming harder all the time to tell whether something is utility or not, and also because schmovie-going is no longer thought of as the art of spotting mis-takes in films, more as the science of predicting them, the idea of utility objects has lost a lot of its importance. There are still plenty around, mind you, but nobody takes them very seriously any more. We prefer to go for certainty in this game. We look for situations where a mis-take is almost a foregone conclusion, and from now on that is where we are heading.

Fated Places

Experience shows there to be certain locations where mis-takes happen more frequently than anywhere else, and scenes taking place near them, in them, behind them or en route to them seem beset by snags. One of these so-called fated places is the hotel. Remember *Silk Stockings, Knock on Wood, The Shining?* Each one is set, in whole or part, in a hotel. Makes you think, doesn't it?

Of course, you might argue that, statistically, things have got to have a better chance of going wrong in a hotel room than, let's say, inside a barrel or up trees. But even taking into account the odds against, it remains an indisputable fact that some surroundings are more vulnerable to error than others, and may even attract goofs for all I know. In the fated places, mis-takes come unbidden.

You don't believe me!

Very well. Ask yourself this question: what happens when you are sitting in a cinema and a character on the screen announces that he is going to check into his hotel? Have you noticed? I'll tell you: immediate unrest. An indefinable malaise sweeps across the first five rows of the stalls. The audience becomes fidgety and tense. People are shifting in their seats, gabbling in whispers. You never knew before what was happening, what it was they were so excited about.

The Police Inspector turns to his junior sergeant and says, 'Let's head back to the hotel, Jenkins, and make s. . .froozhty braalll jushtreeoooo k. . .' His next line and often the one after are all but drowned by the rustle and clicks of jotters and Bics as the schmovie-buffs shift into gear. That one word 'hotel' causes a mental stampede from those in the know. But it needn't be a hotel. That was merely an example. It could just as easily be a barn. . .

> *The Invisible Man* (1933) One winter's night, Claude Rains is trapped inside a burning barn by the police. With no clothes on, he is completely invisible. Yet when he makes a dash to safety through the snow, though obviously barefoot, he leaves clear shoe-prints behind him as he runs.

Or even a public house. . .

> *Genevieve* (1954) In Brighton, before Kenneth More sets off back to London after a vintage car rally, he and his friends call in at a pub for a drink. More appears in the doorway carrying a pint of beer on a tray. He walks

over to the table, but by the time he gets there, the tray has a half-pint glass on it.

You can also include in the list of fated places, volcanoes, African safaris and forbidden Indian mountains. Circuses are cursed for sure – there must be a jinx on every kind of travelling show, from fairs to repertory companies. And anything just anything at all to do with trains is an engraved invitation to the Goof Fairy to cast her vexatious spell.

The Cassandra Crossing (1976) Sophia Loren pays a visit to her ex-husband, played by Richard Harris, in his compartment on board an express train bound for Stockholm. She knocks quietly. 'It's open!' comes from inside. When she slides back the door, you will catch sight of Harris shaving. Ignore him. Look behind him out of the window. As the train moves, the scenery is passing left to right. Loren sits on the bed with her back to that same window, but now the scenery outside is moving right to left. The train is suddenly travelling in the opposite direction.

Live and Let Die (1973) Roger Moore is grappling with an enormous black villain called Tee Hee on a train. As the two of them thrash about from one side of the carriage to the other, Tee Hee lashes out and breaks the window, to reveal that the side of the train they are now on is going a totally different way to the other side.

Avalanche Express (1979) A female terrorist, hi-jacking a train bound for Rotterdam, threatens to let off a grenade unless the guard opens the engine door, which he promptly does. He throws it wide open, but in the exterior shots, as the train rolls on to a bridge, the door is still closed.

Strangely, it is not that directors are somehow more careless when they film in the fated places, it is simply that the probability of error is that much greater. Once you realize this, then schmovie-going begins to lose a little of its randomness. We are one step nearer being able to forecast when a mis-take may happ. . .

BING-BONG!!
Doctor-ctor Brewster-ster. Urgent-tent message-age f-for Doctor-ctor Brewster-ster. Please-ss call-all reception-shun. . .

B-Pictures

You must try and be selective in the kind of films you check. Don't be overly ambitious at the outset: 'Start humble and cheap and work up.'

Ideally, the cost and size of a picture should not have any bearing on the number of mis-takes to be found in it. A $40 million budget is no insurance against error; what that sort of money does is give a film-maker all the resources he needs to do things well. Nothing is ever too much trouble on a megabucks budget. Blessed with the twin luxuries of time and expertise, a director can spend days shooting one scene if he has to. A vital shot that may take up to three months to put together can be taken care of by dispatching a special unit to work on it until they get it right. As we know, perfectionists thrive in these conditions, and big money brings them out in force, with the result that flawless sets are constructed, richly costumed crowd scenes and interiors are designed, together with the most lavish and intricate special effects imaginable. What chance do we stand against all that?

As a consequence, vetting epics for goofs can be a tough challenge. To expect a beginner to wade through three and a half hours of well-made motion-picture to reach one tiny mis-take is asking too much; and sometimes, they can be very tiny indeed:

> *The Big Country* (1958) is an epic Western, following the turgid lives of two warring families in 1880s Texas. A fine film, but one that takes 165 minutes to tell its tale. Unfortunately, it is not until the 163rd minute, when the credits are almost upon us, that we get to see what we're looking for: a strictly 1950s motor-car speeding along a highway in the middle-distance.
>
> *1941* (1979) The power has been switched off in an amusement park, leaving two men stranded precariously on a Ferris Wheel. Wedged into their seat, afraid of tipping over, a young man on the right, old man on the left, neither can move because of the sheer drop below. So they are stuck there for most of the picture until, quite unexpectedly and without reason, they swop sides. The old man is now sitting on the right and the young man on the left.
>
> *Can't Stop the Music* (1980) Valerie Perrine skips through Greenwich Village, New York, licking a two-scoop ice-cream. From shot to shot, quite randomly, the flavours of the scoops change like traffic-lights – chocolate to strawberry to vanilla and back.

All three so minor they are barely worth mentioning, and certainly not worth sitting through the films for. Take them on trust, and as a lesson to leave epics alone until you have come to grips with the technique involved in spotting mis-takes. Instead, go where the pickings are meatier and the mis-takes more plentiful – head straight for the old B-pics, the ones they used to make 30 years ago.

Without doubt, a lot of very untalented people had access to film equipment in the 1950s, when Britain and Hollywood made pictures with low production values almost for the sake of it, churning out clinical backlot Westerns, predictable thrillers and terrible, terrible Cold War science-fiction films by the dozen, as well as all those ten-a-penny out-of-focus romances in which everyone's face became blurred and their eyes watered incessantly whenever they fell in love. It was the Golden Age of conveyor-belt tat, a rich feeding ground for kack-hunters. I mean, where else but in a B-picture could a bomb planted upstairs in the bedroom of a country cottage explode in the front garden *(Pit of Darkness,* 1955), or a police inspector, punched in the right eye during a fight, turn up for work next day with his left eye black and swollen *(The Adventures of PC 49,* 1949)?

I think it's fair to say that most B-pictures are schmovies.

> *Wasp Woman* (1959) Susan Cabot pricks her arm with a hypodermic needle, ready to inject herself with a dose of serum. She presses the plunger on the syringe, the serum goes in one side of her arm and at once squirts out of the other side on to the floor.

> *Devil Girl From Mars* (1954) An alien visitor arrives from space and lands in Scotland. But there are no language problems because she has learned to speak fluent English back on her home planet by tuning in each week to the BBC Home Service.

> *Tarantula* (1955) A dangerous liquid, known to cause hideous deformity in every living thing it touches, is kept securely locked away, and is handled only by experts wearing protective visors and gloves. Professor Leo G.Carroll takes a syringe and draws out a measure of the liquid. He then removes his visor, turns the syringe upside down and, without another thought, gives a couple of quick test squirts into the air to make sure it's working.

> *The Beast From Twenty Thousand Fathoms* (1953) A scientist issues a stern warning to friends about the danger of creatures surviving from prehistoric times, and refers specifically to the Legend of the Loch Lomond Monster.

Around this time, there was a ready market for pictures of negligible merit. Pulp films could be made by any aspiring director with stars in his eyes, a camera in his hand and a film-set in his garage. Produced quickly, like the serials, on pocket-money budgets, they were sent to play out-of-town theatres as bill-fillers, harnessed to a picture of much greater quality, thereby padding out the programme into a whole evening's entertainment.

Provincial cinemas showing these programmes offered a welcome refuge on wet Monday nights to a young audience looking for escapism, fantasy, romance and adventure of the sort that could only be found in the back two rows of the stalls. It didn't matter much to them that the films were rubbish – most of them had not gone to watch the screen anyway, or that the British-made ones were only in dull old black and white. During the years after the war, real life in Britain *was* in black and white for the most part, so this was taken for granted. We could never hope to match the glitz, the glamour, the lavishness and the deep colour of Hollywood's output; they seemed to dominate our playbills, and all we could do was fend them off bravely. These second-rate B-features were our little gesture of defiance.

The local picture-house was a natural forum for lust in those days, and a popular venue for the frustrated and the randy. In the darkness courting couples got the chance to kick off their shoes and canoodle under raincoats, fingering and exploring remote crevices that, up to then, they had only ever seen in photographs. It was an all-round education, learning what to squeeze, what to pull out and tweak, and what not to strike a match on.

Young girls, acutely nervous in ill-fitting frocks and their mother's Sunday earrings, gave themselves to this exercise with an eagerness plainly borne of desperation and relief – relief that this time, at long last, they were about to have their lipstick smudged; this time they had not been overlooked.

Your partner was not necessarily one of your choosing, just the best you could find before you went in. If he was unpleasant to look at, if his breath smelled like old blankets, if he had chapped, indigestible lips and blackheads, it hardly mattered. Once the lights went down, you could turn a blind eye to his blind boils, forget about the constellation of ripening pimples across his forehead, and concentrate on the business in hand.

Elsewhere, the lonely ones, the rejected ones, the disfigured ones – all the 'Don't-you-dare' Dudleys, the 'Hardly-ever' Hildas and the 'Never' Nevilles, slumped impassively into their seats, with no option but to watch the bloody film after all, picking out whatever words they could off the soundtrack over the writhing, sucking, 'Oh Jimmy!' – 'Oh Connie!' – 'Oh Jimmy!' noises wafting across from the back of the stalls.

Afterwards, as the cinema closed, it was another entertainment again, to see these dishevelled snoggers spill, half-asphyxiated, into the rain – women buttoning their coats against the wind, men wiping streaks of make-up off their chapped, indigestible lips – ritualistically swapping addresses and promising dates they knew they wouldn't keep for the following week.

These days, a trip to the cinema is treated with more respect. People pay to watch a film, not to sit and miss it as we did then.

The old B-pictures, the bill-fillers, are still around, only now film distributors have found a new outlet for them. Using a burglar's cunning, they have managed to foist them upon embarrassed television executives, by selling them off as part of some larger package of movies, which is bound to include a handful of eagerly-awaited blockbusters. TV companies buy them, stash them away in the vaults for as long as they can, and then, thinking that we, the audience, will not want to sit through numerous clinical backlot Westerns, predictable thrillers and terrible, terrible Cold War science-fiction films, they slip them as quietly as possible into the schedules on wet Monday afternoons when they hope we'll be out, or at midnight while we're asleep.

Nevertheless, I do urge you to track down as many of them as you can, if only to familiarize yourself with the weary old storylines, plot devices and lines of dialogue that turn up time and again in film after film. In the end, you too will feel the same way as the rest of us, I'm sure: that originality in motion pictures died finally around the end of the 1960s. Nothing is new any more. Even new films are not new, merely variations on something else that has gone before; each element in them, each visual effect, each twist, joke and development can be traced back to a hundred or so similar films in the past, and beyond those to another hundred. Out of this non-stop sameness comes one fact of which we are sure, there are definite rules for making movies, strict formulae catering for every possible contingency that may arise on the screen. After years spent making films and watching them, a director knows the rules instinctively. They restrict him in everything he does. He finds himself repeating what his predecessors did, referring back to how they overcame the problems he is facing now, and doing the same thing. And repetition is the schmovie-buff's greatest ally in spotting mis-takes. Schmovie-buffs know the rules as well.

War-films have a set all to themselves. So do musicals, thrillers and fantasy adventures. But it does not stop there. Behind these lie scores more, smaller, individual guidelines, governing specific items within each film, from weapons to dance routines to thunderstorms to fire-extinguishers. If a picture has a bar-room brawl in it somewhere, then there are rules for that, too, and for Indian uprisings, feasts and orgies, car-chases – everything you can think of.

They tell a director when he may or may not show sailors drinking in a night-club, for instance; which way a skull should face while it is in shot; that the lawman in a Western must always ride into town with a corpse thrown over his saddle; who would make the best victim for mindless homicide; which of the survivors on a drifting life-raft should be the first to die. Petty things possibly, but together they make up a body of ground-rules that, given the correct circumstances, the director will stick to religiously, and which has come to be known throughout the industry as the Cliché Code.

Picture it as a small book if you like – rather dog-eared from over-use – divided up into a hundred or more sections, each dealing with a different component in any film (the story, the characters, special effects, sets, etc.), and including on every page, a selection of tips and tricks-of-the-trade drawn from over 60 years of feature-film making.

All the old knackered plotlines are in there: the amnesiac searching for two weeks lost from his life; the man accused of a murder he didn't commit, who sets out to prove his innocence; the identical bags switched in an airport lounge with hilarious consequences; the sheriff who runs from the jailhouse to the saloon, from the saloon to the bank, from the bank to the stable, from the stable to the barn, then throws himself behind a trough, under continuous heavy gunfire and doesn't get hit once; the dizzy hoofer with a sweet face and thin ankles, who turns up on Broadway, sporting a hold-all full of tutus, a heartful of dreams and a headful of not much, and makes it to the top of the dancing tree in an hour and ten minutes; the army private who bears a striking resemblance to Adolf Hitler, and who is asked to take his place to foil an assassination plot – 'No, no, I won't do it. I absolutely refuse. The answer's no!' – and the next thing you know, he is goosestepping about the mess in a sticky-tape moustache, shouting, 'Gotterdammerung!' 'Rechts stehen!' and 'Hände hoch!'

Not so much knackered plotlines perhaps, more like old friends who regularly come to visit – the sort of friends who have visited so regularly of late, you are beginning to tire of their company.

Looked at broadly, the Cliché Code is a recyclopaedia, spewing out for the umpteenth time ideas that were considered old-hat three decades ago, but which still continue to be used. Some dip into it sparingly, falling back on its advice only as a valuable time-saver. Others lift entire stories from it wholesale. For the director low on inspiration, who has run out of barrels to scrape, it is a handy back-pocket companion, helping him to cope with those darker moments that can grip a film in mid-production, when he finds he has wandered up an artistic cul-de-sac, with not an idea in his head of what to do next. It will tell him in an instant everything he needs to know, from how a tramp should be dressed in a film, right down to the best ways of identifying his characters.

Before we go any further, a quick warning. I hate to lace every turn of our little game with these warnings, but so much of the theory of schmovie-going is open to misinterpretation. The films we use to illustrate the way in which the Code works are just that, illustrations, and no more. We cannot tell whether the directors had a copy to hand when they made them. For our purposes in this book, it is sufficient that the rules have been followed – whether a film-maker did so by instinct or by reference to the Cliché Code is immaterial. We can't suggest that he used it, because we simply don't know.

Identifying the Characters

No plot of any kind can properly take shape until the characters involved in it have been introduced to the audience. At its most basic, this means that every person who is important to the story must be called *by their name* within 60 seconds of our first meeting them. No picture should stumble over something so simple as this, but you would be astonished how many do. And when they do, we are waiting, sitting, watching, itching to catch them out.

The name-for-name trick works efficiently, but it can be overdone.

> *The Tuttles of Tahiti* (1941) The lead character is a man called Chester, and you are never left in a moment's doubt about this, because he is called Chester at least 25 times in the first 7 minutes.

> *The Flame and the Arrow* (1950) Burt Lancaster plays a jester called Dardo, a fact you are unlikely to forget since the rest of the cast call his name 82 separate times in a picture that is only 88 minutes long altogether.

Writers have never really cared much for this approach, and have therefore devised various ways over the years of sidestepping it. The Code lists them in full, and once you know what they are, the whole naming process takes on a cheery parlour-game quality as you try and guess in each case which one they will use this time. Will it be the prominently positioned name-block on the office desk? Or the cut-out letters stuck on the door? Or the excited postman rapping at the window: 'Parcel for Mrs Williams. Are *you* Mrs Williams?' 'Yes, I sure am!' Or the butler advancing into the library: 'Professor Faltskog to see you, sir.' Or even. . .

BING-BONG!!
Doctor-ctor Brewster-ster t-to reception-shun immediately-iately.
Urgent-tent message-age f-for Doctor-ctor Brewster-ster. . .

Out of a small group of concerned men in white coats with glasses, one will peel away and make for the nearest phone. *That* is Doctor Brewster, and that is also the method film-makers are most proud of, the public address system. They use it all the time. Characters in films are forever reporting to information or check-in desks to collect messages, not because there is really a message to be collected, you understand, but to single them out from the crowd, to bring them to our attention.

The usual way in spy films is for the face of each main character to be projected on to a screen before a huddle of secret agents in a darkened room. A very clumsy and long-winded way of doing it, and highly tedious for the audience. Far better is if the character you are introducing is an actor, then it's a breeze. Either stand a board in the theatre foyer with his name and picture on it, and the slash 'Tonite' pasted across, or, even easier, stick his name up in lights. This works a treat – sometimes.

> *The Bandwagon* (1953) Cyd Charisse plays a ballet dancer called Gabrielle Gerard. But when she stars in a show at the Alcott Theatre in New York, her name is misspelt 'Girard' in lights outside. Soon afterwards, a copy of the programme for the show is held up to the camera. Her name is spelled correctly on the cast-list – Gerard. Alas, they have now got the name of the theatre wrong. It says Alcott on the canopy outside, but Stratton on the programme!

Having gone to the trouble of establishing which role a particular actor is playing, the last thing a director then wants is for that same actor to be called by his or her real name while the cameras are rolling.

> *Grease* (1979) John Travolta's car at the drive-in theatre has 'John' finger-painted into the dirt on the door, even though he plays a high-school kid and mechanic called Danny in the picture. When the vehicles were being allocated, this was clearly the easiest way of identifying which one was his.

At the Earth's Core (1976) Peter Cushing and Doug McClure are on the run from a man-in-a-suit-monster. While Cushing is being chased up a tree, McClure backs away slowly, and a dull voice from behind the camera calls, 'Dougie!' Hearing his name, McClure looks round, takes instructions about what to do next, viz 'run off', and runs off.

Meet Me in St Louis (1944) This is the all-time classic. Judy Garland boards a trolley-bus for the St Louis fair. She hasn't far to go, only a few miles, but realizes that she will get there a darned sight quicker if she sings a song about it. At the time they were filming this sequence, while Miss Garland was singing 'The Trolley Song', a friend of hers walked on to the set behind the camera and, thinking this was just a dress rehearsal, shouted, 'Hi, Judy!' Apart from a slight glimmer of concern, the interruption barely registered on her face and she carried on singing. Indeed, so good was her cover-up that the scene has been left in the picture as it stands, 'Hi Judy!' and all.

Names and symbols of any sort can be useful in keeping the continuity juices flowing between one scene and another, or one part of the film and the next – or not.

Diamonds Are Forever (1971) A hearse belonging to a commercial cremation company, Slumber Inc, is parked outside a hanger at Los Angeles International Airport. On the door is the company logo, a large feather sloping downwards towards the back wheel. The hearse is driven away across the desert to the mortuary – not far, but in the short space of time it takes to get there, the feather changes direction and on arrival, is sloping downwards *away* from the wheel.

Knock on Wood (1954) A sticker glued to the side of a delivery van, reads 'Carr & Brookes Exclusive Menswear' and slopes upwards left to right while the van is parked in an alleyway, but downwards left to right when it pulls out into the street.

Operation Crossbow (1965) The Germans have been testing out long-range flying bombs, firing them from special ramps in secret locations. So far, they have not

> had too much success. Due to an as yet undiscovered fault, each bomb tends to veer off-course seconds after its launch, and hit a tree. The first bomb on the ramp has M23 stencilled on the tail. They fire it, it veers off-course and hits a tree – completely destroyed. Not to be defeated, they try another, or rather, the same one, because the bomb that's just gone up in flames is back on the ramp again, with M23 on the tail, but only for a few seconds, then the number is changed hastily to M28.

Do be careful, though, not to become so sidetracked by the identification process that you let a genuine mis-take slip by, unnoticed.

> *For A Few Dollars More* (1965) Bounty-hunter Lee Van Cleef arrives in the town of Tucumcari on the trail of an outlaw, Guy Calloway. According to the wanted poster on the station wall, the price on Calloway's head is $1,000, but Calloway himself has added a couple of extra noughts in crayon to that figure, making it $100,000. Van Cleef rips down the poster, rolls it up and stuffs it inside his coat, then makes for the hotel where the outlaw is staying. Outside Calloway's room, Van Cleef unrolls the poster and slides it under the door to announce his arrival, but the extra noughts have now disappeared, and the reward is down to $1,000 again – a few dollars less in fact.

Such a glaring oversight, too! Maria Luisa Rosen, the continuity girl on this one, must be turning in her grave – if she's dead, that is.

Names

The Cliché Code is very strict on names. You can't call any old Tom, Dick or Harry, Tom, Dick or Harry. The name you give to a character has got to say something about him, it must fit the personality.

As a matter of protocol, for example, raw cowhands, loggers and rough and raunchy pioneering-types are never called Julian or Beverley. Heroes have to be die-hard and intrepid-sounding. They must be given clipped and masculine names, such as Brock, Griff, Jim, Tom, Hank, Dirk, Marshall, Curtis, Chip, Dale or Trent. Kip Carlton, Ted Banner or Ben Tanner, now *that's* a tough-guy's name, something firm and dependable, a broad-shouldered 'no-funny-business-here' kind of name, one that slaps you across the back when you hear it, that says 'Let me help you' or 'You stand back, I'll handle this'.

Even before you meet him you know Kip Carlton could wrestle wild cheetahs if he had to, tear a telephonist in half with his bare hands, that he could leap out of bed one morning and lay waste an entire forest before lunchtime. He likes his liquor strong and his women weak, and he always knows just how many bullets the other fella has got left in his gun. You wouldn't hesitate to let this guy take your son to the lavatory.

Only a damn-fool writer would call the Sheriff of Fractured Jaw Crispen, Denzil or Jocelyn and expect ever to work again, unless the name was shortened in the script to Chris, Den or Joss. The same for Beverley: Bev Cranshaw sounds fine, but for convention's sake, Beverley Cranshaw had better be his neice from Wyoming, or else.

If you are a director trying to find a name for a butcher, then my advice is to call him Sam. Everyone else does. The Code insists that Sam makes a good butcher. Bartenders should be called Jerry, Joey or, if you're really desperate, Philippe, although in Westerns barmen can be called anything you want just so long as, when we first see them, they are standing behind the bar rubbing a whisky glass with a towel.

Ralph and Eugene are the all-time nerd names. Ralph has a gaping mouth, wears cream-rimmed National Health spectacles and carries a satchel at 32. Eugene traditionally has the wit and drive of a sideboard leg and takes holiday photos with the lens cap on. Surprisingly, some of the best doormen are called Ralph, but that is merely a quirk in the system.

British murder mysteries are always solved by a police inspector with an upstanding solid name – Lynch, Clinner, Bell, Chubb or Tate. In thrillers, everyone manages to say the inspector's name at least once before the case is solved, so it has to be snappy and memorable and must stand up to endless repetition. Any wishy-washy non-committal names are reserved for the wishy-washy non-committal sergeants who pad around behind them, sucking pastilles and making rough jottings. They are best called Barker, Palmer, Parker, Benson, Dobson, Jenkins or Johnson.

In American detective dramas the cops in the police department are simply Bob, Joe or Frank. Their wives are Betty if it's just a TV movie, Mary if it's destined for a cinema release. Lou is the overweight sergeant in the San Francisco homicide squad, the one who gets shot on his last case and dies, leaving the rest of the cast to spend what is left of the picture hunting down his killer. Wally brings the coffee to Bob, Joe and Frank while they're on duty in the daytime. At night, Frank will volunteer to fetch it himself. There should always be a pot-bellied Irish simpleton called Mulligan, O'Malley or O'Grady on point duty, who continually throws back his cap in dismay to scratch his head, and splutters a half-sentence when he sees some crime being committed: 'Well, I'll be. . .'

Bud makes a great gas station proprietor. He will always wipe his hands on his overalls as he walks towards a car. His mechanic is called

Danny, although this is no cliché, this is hard fact. Every American car mechanic I've ever met was called Danny. Dannies wipe their fingers on a dirty rag before shaking hands.

Martha is the name given to the mother-figure in Westerns, the one with the comely reassuring bust, who stands in the doorway of the ranchhouse tying and retying her apron and waiting for her hair to turn grey. She spends all day every day boiling up pots of coffee on the hob, scattering feed for the chickens from a pail, baking fresh batches of oatcakes, and looking after little Billy while the menfolk are out breaking steers or burying Kip Carlton. She is also the first to be slaughtered in a massacre.

Oh, and before I forget, little boys in American films are always called Billy. I can't rule out Robbie or Bobby here, but in most cases, they follow the Code and go for Billy.

Leo is the swinging single, the balding, menopausal, good-time guy in the bright yellow Hawaiian shirt and flared slacks – either he never married or has been divorced five times – and now lives two doors along the landing from our hero, so that he can pop round to provide a little light relief when the story takes a serious turn. Leo holds noisy bikini parties every night, where under-age girls in cheeky swimsuits, with hair that has an exaggerated curl all the way round the bottom as though it has been fashioned in a fibreglass mould, twist and jive into the small hours to old Hammond organ demonstration records.

Carol is a middle-aged basket-case with a thousand hang-ups ranked in order of severity for conversation-purposes, and has just driven her fiftieth shrink into a special home. She is either one of Leo's more troublesome ex-girlfriends or his fourth wife, who sits in the airing-cupboard downing pills between swigs of bourbon, and whose breath would take the pattern off your china.

Candy is head-nympho at Leo's parties. Debbies are usually sex-starved for some reason. Isabels always wear lace and have their hair in ringlets down the back. Mexican prostitutes are best called Juanita.

Pirates are known by the name of their most recent and most conspicuous disability – Peg-Leg or Dead-Eye, though this never becomes so probing as to stretch to more personal ailments: they do not therefore get called Dislodged-Retina Dick, Strawberry-Rash Pete or Low-Sperm-Count Dan.

Working-class housewives in British comedies are named Glad, Peg, Winn or Else.

Johnny is a dangerous convict on the loose after serving only part of his sentence. Everybody in the US armed forces is called Kowalski.

British criminal gangs and prisoner-of-war camp inmates share the same range of names: Corky, Dusty, Chalky, Smudger, Bingo, Nobby, Pins, Taff, Paddy, Jock, Fingers, Eddie and Blinker. Blinker is the guy in the escape tunnel with the tea-spoon and the billy-can who is buried in a freak rockfall. Bingo dresses as a washerwoman and makes an escape attempt in a passing haycart. Smudger is brought in to forge ID cards and passports. Pins can run up a faultless Nazi Kommandant's uniform in twelve hours, using just two blankets, some chocolate wrappers and the mess curtains. Dusty, meanwhile, keeps look-out while Jock, Taff and Paddy chat in quaint accents to please foreign viewers, and pull the stove or the vaulting horse back over the tunnel entrance.

Scene-Setting I

To the harassed director with a fat tale to tell and only 90 minutes in which to tell it, the laborious task of setting the scene for his story can be a real drag – an essential one because an audience does have to be told where the action takes place, in which country, city, street, etc., but still a drag for all that. He knows that every inch of the film given over to scene-setting may be eating into valuable plot-time elsewhere, and therefore the faster it can be cleared out of the way, the better for everyone.

Schmovie-buffs generally show little interest in what has become a fairly mechanical process. However, there is one small corner of it which absolutely fascinates us, and that is when a film is set in one country, but shot in another.

These days movie-making is a truly international business. Films are made on locations all over the world. If an American producer wishes to take his actors to Paris for some vital scenes then, budget permitting, he will do so. If some part of a British film is set in Rio de Janeiro, likely as not the camera crew will go to Rio to make it. Audiences expect it of them. Our standards are very high, and we won't be fobbed off with actors posing in front of a giant blow-up photograph of the Coliseum in Rome, or the World Trade Centre in New York. But this was not the case in the fifties. At that time, it was rare for Hollywood to come to Europe. Europe invariably had to be taken lock, stock and cliché to Hollywood.

After all – so went the reasoning – why should they pay vast sums for the cast and crew to fly to London for three weeks on expenses, when they could send a runner to the studio archive to dig out that old piece of stock footage – the one with the picture postcard view of the Houses of Parliament on it, taken while Big Ben was chiming the quarter-hour? If they tagged this scene on to the front of the picture they were making, who was to say that they hadn't spent months on location in England shooting the entire movie there? Not absolutely logical, but you can understand its attraction.

First, it meant instant recognition. Cinema-goers everywhere knew at once that this was London, not because they had ever been there, but because they had seen this same shot in so many other films. And second, audiences were a darned sight more gullible then, ready to accept just about anything they were shown. They took this version of England as being for real, not as a snippet of worn-out archive film followed by a wholly risible plywood London-replica built on the studio backlot in California. Props had been shipped in specially, all the English actors they could find had been rounded up for supporting roles, and the whole thing was just perfect! In reality, it was a perfect reproduction of what Hollywood thought England looked like, and as we know Hollywood's vision of England bears no resemblance to the real thing.

Royal Wedding (1951) 'London' in this one has American fire-hydrants in the streets and an English bus – the only one they had – that passes backwards and forwards across the set, travelling as far as it can go one way, then turning around and coming back.

13 Frightened Girls (1963) In 'Belgravia' there are brown pillar boxes on the kerb, and American street-lamps lining the road.

Knock on Wood (1954) Danny Kaye is still on the run from Scotland Yard after finding the dead body in his wardrobe. He takes refuge in a car-showroom in the heart of 'London' – but all the cars in the traffic outside the window are left-hand drive.

The Invisible Man (1933) A 'British Police Station' has the American words 'Police Department' spelled out on the door.

Merry Andrew (1958) Danny Kaye is cycling along an 'English country lane' in central London, behind a red double-decker bus bound for Piccadilly Circus. The bus is on the right-hand side of the road to begin with, the American side, and all the cars coming the other way, that can't get by because of the bus, the bike and the truck with the camera on it, are being forced on to the grass verge behind some bushes in the background, to join the road again further on.

13 Frightened Girls (1963) A car driving down another 'English country lane' at night passes a line of American mail-boxes at a T-junction on three separate occasions.

Fear of the confusion caused by this crude brand of scene-setting has taken such a grip on film-makers nowadays that any picture set in London, even those *made* in London but intended for international distribution, must have in them most, if not all, of the eight standard 'you can tell it's London because. . .' features.
Tick them off as you spot them:

1. The bright red pillar box.
2. The bright red telephone box.
3. The bright red double-decker bus.
4. The black London cab.
5. The courteous British bobby on his beat, who salutes the old folks and tells little children the time and only hits criminals.
6. A man in a bowler hat with a brolly (regardless of the weather, note!) who says, 'Pip pip, old chap' to the bobby on the beat.
7. An old butler with tunnel-nostrils and a scornful look, but otherwise as near to Sir John Gielgud or Sir Alec Guinness as they can make him.
8. And, of course, plenty of paupers: Hollywood loves the British working classes – they're such jolly people, always singing and making do, and whether they are freckled urchins, knife-grinders or Covent Garden flower sellers in wide-brimmed hats, as most of them are, they all have an impenetrable accent of the sort that only exists in films and which makes them sound like drunken Melbourne hairdressers.

To the American mind, every hotel, office, bar and restaurant in London has a clear view over the rooftops to the Houses of Parliament, and is within earshot of Big Ben chiming the quarter-hour. Meals are eaten in the shadow of St Paul's Cathedral or Tower Bridge. Any important rendezvous is arranged for Trafalgar Square. And, as we know, buses are always on their way to Piccadilly Circus.

> *Expresso Bongo* (1959) The view across London from a balcony at the Dorchester Hotel appears to have been pieced together from layers of chipboard, painted to look like buildings, then positioned one behind the other to give that special feeling of depth and distance only planks of wood can convey. This appalling timber vista is made even less credible by the fact that someone has been messing with the layout between shots, and changing the buildings around. The first time we are allowed a glimpse off the balcony, Westminster Abbey stands to the left of the Houses of Parliament. The next time we look out, the Abbey has moved over and now stands to the right of the Houses of Parliament.

If the film has been made on location, they are never slow to remind you. All car journeys across London, however brief, take the driver along the Mall, past Buckingham Palace, around Trafalgar Square, then up Fleet Street, with St Paul's clearly framed in the back window, no matter which direction he is travelling in. Everyone is prepared to break off a busy schedule to take a wild extravagant detour around the best, most well-known tourist landmarks for the benefit of the audience, and for precisely the same reason that rampaging monsters and aliens from other worlds only ever attack tourist spots – the Capitol Building in Washington, the Empire State Building, The Taj Mahal.

> *Gorgo* (1960) A monster wades up the Thames in London ripping the top off Tower Bridge as she goes. Yet minutes later, when she wades back down again, Tower Bridge is completely undamaged.

France suffers a similar indignity to England. For Paris, the scene is always set using stock archive footage of the Eiffel Tower overlaid with a sickly slithering accordion accompaniment. For a scene set elsewhere in France, the Code dictates that there should be a large Dubonnet advertisement somewhere well in shot *(Dunkirk,* 1958; *Tarnished Heroes,* 1961), and by rights, there should also be an overweight onion-seller riding by, ch-chinging his bicycle bell, and dressed in French national costume – the black beret tilted at a naughty angle, and the stripy shirt. He should be shouting schoolboy French to pedestrians: 'Où est la gare?' 'Jean-Paul est allé au jardin-public!' with a degree of urgency that suggests he knows what he is talking about.

Before we dismiss archive material outright, though, I should point out that it does serve some purpose occasionally.

Besides all those flat scenic shots of the world's greatest postcard views, the archives have a smattering of disasters – volcanoes erupting, floods, earthquakes, ships sinking – footage that would take special-effects men weeks of work and thousands of dollars to recreate in the studio; plus miles and miles of old newsreel film left over from the war. Any one of these can be brought up from the cellars and spliced into a picture that needs beefing up with a bit of spectacle, and whose budget won't run to having the scene shot especially for it. All a director has to do is ensure that the shots either side of the stock film match up with it. That's all. . .

> *Retreat, Hell!* (1952) Prior to a beach assault by the US marines in Korea, the crew of one of the ships is called up on deck. As they scramble to their various positions, the men are wearing life-jackets – but only in long-shot. Close up, the real marines are replaced by actors who have not been issued with life-jackets.

Although when they come to disembark we are back to the stock-footage, and they are wearing jackets again.

The Bermuda Triangle (1978) A stock galleon heaving and dipping in mile-high waves, has a brown mast – except for when the actors stand on the deck, when the mast is white.

Operation Crossbow (1965) When the Nazi flying bombs, targeted on London, reach the South Coast of England, the only defence we have against them, it seems, is some stock artillery footage of a man at Dover trying to shoot them down. And you would hardly notice that they'd used stock footage at all, I'm sure, if it were not for the fact that the shot is grainy and scratched and in black and white, while the scenes either side of it are full colour.

Carry on Again, Doctor (1969) A stock hurricane hits an exotic island, almost tearing the palm trees out of the ground. In the next shot, somewhere on the island, the flag on a pole next to a medical centre is hanging limp, with no breeze to ripple it.

A shortage of cash is not the only reason for keeping a picture studio-bound. At times, it may be more sensible to shoot important scenes on the backlot to allow the director greater control over something that might be difficult to film effectively on location, a dance-routine, for example. . .

The Young Ones (1961) During the song 'No-one for meee but Nickeee', teenager-in-love Carole Grey prances along a 'London' street built on the backlot at Elstree Studios. This is 'The Elstreet', a line of plaster façades – house-fronts and shops, with little else behind them but waste-ground and trees. Take a look at the wall between the police station and the shop next to it. You will find a chink in the brickwork, a gap where the two buildings don't quite meet, and through it you'll see the back of the set: scaffolding propping up the wall and debris scattered across the ground. It would appear that they have tried to hide the join by standing a 'you can tell it's London because. . .' bright red telephone box in front of it – but, luckily, without much success.

. . .or a chase.

> *The First Great Train Robbery* (1978) Wayne Sleep plays a small-time villain in 1855, on the run after reporting Sean Connery, a big-time crook and con-man, to the police. He skips through a series of dark and twisting Victorian alleyways, and down a very authentic-looking London high street built at Pinewood Studios, and finally into a little tunnel, the end of which is blocked off by a gate that, through a fortuitous oversight, has been left slightly ajar – to reveal a modern, dark blue carpenter's van, parked 'out of sight' behind the set.

No matter how convincing they try to make the set look, there are still a couple of ways it can reveal itself for what it really is – a fake.

> *20,000 Leagues Under the Sea* (1954) In 1868, talk around the offices of the Great Western Steam Packet Co is of a mysterious sea-creature attacking ships and sinking them. Professor Aronnax is nevertheless booking a voyage across the haunted stretch of ocean to prove this tale is mere hokum. The view out of the office-window is an elaborate backdrop of numerous old sailing ships moored in San Francisco Harbour. So when the Professor walks outside and stands in front of the same building, those ships should then be *reflected* in the window-pane, shouldn't they? But no, what is actually reflected is a giant billboard, some trees and a man adjusting a lamp.

> *Cleopatra* (1963) Queen of Egypt Elizabeth Taylor arrives in Rome aboard a massive sphynx, pulled by two columns of slaves. As they pass underneath the magnificent triumphal arch, constructed especially for the film, the tubular steel scaffolding holding it up at the back casts a criss-cross shadow over the top of the sphynx's head, and behind one of the smaller arches I'm sure you can see the scaffolding itself poking through.

History is always tricky. The authentic period feel of a picture, created so meticulously, often at great cost, can easily be ruined by just one lapse. That's all it takes to break the spell.

> *The Crimson Pirate* (1952) is set in eighteenth-century Spain. After their ship, *The Crimson Lady,* is captured by the wicked Baron Gruder, the crew are scooped up in the rigging and left to swing from the mast, all hands and legs and cutlasses. But if you take your eyes off them for a moment and look behind them across the bay there is a modern-day ocean liner, large as life, with its stern towards the camera, cruising out to sea. If you miss it the first time round, don't worry, because it makes three separate appearances in ten minutes. It looked to be the *Queen Mary* from where I was sitting, but I had my head in my hands at the time, so I can't be 100 per cent sure.

Perhaps it is because film-makers try so hard to recreate the past that schmovie-goers dig so deep into historical pictures to find evidence of the present.

Civilization has advanced to such an extent now that any place that lacks the joint conveniences of fast highways, aircraft lanes and a Burger King is probably not worth filming in anyway. Wherever they take their cameras to shoot a period piece, you can bet that the twentieth century will never be too far away, whether it be a jet-trail in the sky *(Dracula – Prince of Darkness,* 1965); a TV aerial on a prison roof in 1865 *(Mysterious Island,* 1961); a Friedland plastic bell-push in 1940 *(Battle of Britain,* 1969); a zip in the back of Maid Marion's dress *(Sword of Sherwood Forest,* 1960); a vaccination mark in a man's arm in ancient mythical Greece (*Atlantis, The Lost Continent,* 1961); a British GPO manhole cover in 1870's Massachusetts *(Heaven's Gate,* 1980); the mention of ball-bearings in prehistoric times *(The Wild Women of Wongo,* 1958); a modern luxury yacht standing in the middle of landlocked Belgium in 1944 *(Battle of the Bulge,* 1965); or even a rumoured electric Boots the Chemists sign in 1939 *(Goodbye, Mr Chips,* 1969).

> *El Cid* (1961) The action takes place in Spain around the start of the eleventh century, and the question that has hung over this film for more than 20 years is: 'Is there a lorry in it or not?' Charlton Heston (El Cid) has been shot in the chest during a battle, and has retired into the walled city of Valencia. The armies on the beach outside march to the city, chanting, 'The Cid is dead! The Cid is dead!' And as they storm towards us, a small white truck winds slowly around a bend in the road on the hillside behind them. 'What, you mean that widgy-wee dot on the horizon?' Yes, I know it's small, but it's also motorized, it's moving and, most of all, *it's there!*

A more satisfactory example is to be found in *The Wonderful World of the Brothers Grimm* (1962), a well-made piece set in nineteenth-century Bavaria, at the time when Jacob and Wilhelm Grimm were writing their fairy tales.

> Following a huge row, the two brothers stand together on the banks of the Rhine, about to part company. So engrossed are they in their goodbyes that they miss the distinctly 1960s holiday traffic speeding along a road on the far side of the river. A white car first, which someone has identified as a Volkswagen (though on a normal viewing it is hard to tell), and once that has slipped out of view, a second car takes over and returns the other way.

The only time you might feel the slightest bit sorry for a director is when he has taken the greatest care to keep all latter-day objects well out of camera-range, only then to be foiled by a totally unexpected reflection.

> *Pennies From Heaven* (1981) In 1934 Chicago, Steve Martin opens the door of a vintage car and as it swings back a modern Bedford van, parked out of shot, is reflected in the window.

> *Chitty Chitty Bang Bang* (1968) You need to be quick to see this, so be ready to look when I say 'Now'. Caractacus Potts (Dick Van Dyke) has built a flying-car, a gleaming chrome machine, which he decides to test-drive through the local village. He takes with him his two blond-haired children, the sort of teething saccharine-smiled cuties peculiar to musicals, and the sort you want to cuff, and cuff hard! As they ride, they sing to the car: 'You're sleek as a thoroughbred, your seats are a feather-bed. . .' NOW! That's your cue to look into the chrome on the car's bonnet. Remember, these are Victorian times: in the side of the car are reflected three residential caravans resembling Porta-kabins, standing on a slope leading down to the road, and looking suspiciously like the trailers that might be used by costume, make-up and other production units when they film on location.

Anti-Schmovie Devices

Since we know that mis-takes happen quite irrespective of the degree of care taken to avoid them, there would seem to be little or no point in directors going to great lengths to prevent them. However, when they do make an effort to gloss over a goof, even though it may be totally ineffectual, we call this an anti-schmovie device.

It includes highly shiny surfaces discreetly misted over so that they won't reflect the camera.

> *When Eight Bells Toll* (1971) Anthony Hopkins takes a helicopter ride up to a castle in the Scottish Highlands. When it lands, the pilot pulls back the door and shows us that the raised visor on his helmet has been 'dulled' to make it less reflective, which is a good move on the film-maker's part. Shame it doesn't work. The pilot then moves his head in such a way that both the camera and the microphone are reflected quite clearly in the visor.

Or it may be that a utility object had to be removed during filming to avert an 'incident'.

> *Dentist on the Job* (1961) In this one, a soap manufacturer is filming a commercial for its Pink Pierre bath-soap. The model (Shirley Eaton) has been immersed in a foam bath on a mock-up bathroom set, that has pillars, balustrades, festooned curtains and a dressing-table with three mirrors on top. Bob Monkhouse, standing in the wings, accidentally knocks against a wind-machine, switching it on and blowing all the suds out of the bath. Miss Eaton leaps to her feet with a towel around her chest, and immediately sexists in the audience tend to let their eyes wander casually towards the dressing-table. Since she has her back to it, the mirrors should reflect her bare bottom quite clearly. Well, this certainly would have been so, had the film-crew not cottoned on to this before we did, and hastily removed the mirrors between shots!

Basically, an anti-schmovie device is any trick a film-maker uses to prevent the audience spotting a mis-take, but which only serves to draw your attention to what has gone wrong. No blame attaches to anyone doing this, incidentally; it is perfectly acceptable, and directors should be commended for trying it. That phone-box standing up against the chink in the wall in *The Young Ones* may very well have been just such a device, and you'll find a good scene-setting example in *Grease* (1979):

> The scene: Rydell High School, America, the mid-fifties, right after the 'Summer Nights' number. In the schoolyard, a small group of junior girls have been very carefully positioned to stand between two concrete pillars and so block out the view we might otherwise have of a stream of seventies' sports and saloon-cars flashing along a four-lane highway behind them. Unfortunately, these girls get chatting, and start to play and joke and run about back there so that, without realizing, they move away from their specially-chosen spot between the pillars, giving us a clear view of the freeway after all.

Going Places

Before we leave the subject of scene-setting, a word about the stringent guidelines laid down by the Cliché Code on how actors may travel from place to place.

The method varies according to the length of the journey:

1. *Continental Travel.* The fastest way to travel between continents is undoubtedly by map. It was always more convenient for a director to rip page 27 out of a primary school atlas, and then draw dotted lines across it to connect up the various countries en route than it was for him to show us the finer, more tedious details of the journey itself – actors climbing off and on planes, walking through customs etc. This makes it ideal for long sea-voyages, overland odysseys, camel trains or pioneering expeditions to the poles. It cuts out weeks of unnecessary trekking and is guaranteed to take the characters to their destination faster than any conventional means. Pirates in olden days travelled extensively by map, which partly explains why the technical term for it within the industry is 'the travelling mappe process'.

2. *Country to Country.* Journeys between countries are best completed, as in real life, by aeroplane. But do make sure that the plane you see in the air is the same one that lands at the airport.

> *Broadway* (1942) A TWA plane on its way to New York City has six windows down the side while it is in flight, but seven when it lands.

Showing an aeroplane touching down on a runway in the country of destination is usually quite enough to set the scene, provided it taxis to a halt somewhere near a large sign with the name of the airport on it, on the basis that every audience contains a sizeable Dimwit Element, made up of people so vacant or retarded that they must have the most elementary points underlined in red three times or bawled at them through a loud-hailer. Therefore, nothing is ever left to chance. Everywhere will always be clearly signposted so that you don't get lost.

NB. If the plane is shown taking off rather than landing then some part of the story will almost certainly unfold during the flight.

3. *Between Cities*. There has only ever been one real choice for this, and that's the stock passenger train that charges straight at the camera with a searing whistle and some diddly-dum diddly-dum music. The camera is always positioned low down, either on the track itself or close by.

> *The Jolson Story* (1946) On his first tour of the States, Al Jolson's concerts are all joined together by means of a stock express train, each performance leading into the next, carried along by the train hurtling down the track at the camera. On one occasion the train screams past a little shed and a telegraph pole, then disappears off the left side of the picture. Later, when they try this trick again, and when Jolson has moved further afield across the country, they use what looks like the same train on the same track, only this time a couple of hundred yards further on, and it passes the little shed and the telegraph pole yet again.

> *The Benny Goodman Story* (1955) The venues played by Benny when he is touring with Ben Pollack's band are linked by a chuffing train wheezing along a track. But every hall they play seems somewhat familiar. The stage is facing a different way, but the curtains are the same, and you'd swear the same people are slow-stepping in front of the stage in every town: one young lady in a violent red dress is especially noticeable on a couple of occasions, dancing with her boyfriend in a light grey suit. Either they are playing in different corners of the same soundstage, pursued by a fanatical band of extras who would follow them to the end of the set, if necessary, or they. . .no, there is no 'or', I'm pretty sure they go absolutely nowhere on the whole tour!

4. *Short-hops.* Included in this are trips down the street, around the corner, across the park, or to the local fair. All the director needs is a brief 'skip and a jump' sequence to fill a gap, and to take his characters where they need to go to continue the narrative. The best way to achieve it, as we already know, is by song. Travelling on the back of a song is a quick, breezy and undemanding way to get from A to B.

> *A Run for Your Money* (1949) It is Hollywood's firm belief that Welsh people sing at the top of their voices all day long, wherever they are, whatever they are doing. And nothing the British film industry had done has ever dampened this laughable misconception. A number of miners take a trip to London from Welsh Wales. They are only a small group, but no matter whether they are walking down the street, standing on the football terraces, stumbling along train corridors, and regardless of whether they are outnumbered by women and children, they still sing with the skill, volume and resonance of a full male-voice choir.

Time for more warnings, about travel on this occasion. First, and this might seem an obvious point, if the characters in a film decide to travel, do make sure that they go somewhere.

> *Carry on Cruising* (1962) The cruise ship *SS Happy Wanderer* takes a tour from Spain to Italy and North Africa. But whenever it pulls in to dock, it doesn't matter which port it is supposed to be, the ship always moors up against the same quayside with the same tree standing on it.

> *Man About the House* (1974) A businessman climbs into a taxi outside Thames Television Studios in London, tells the driver to take him to Thames Television and, in all seriousness, rides around the block and steps out in exactly the same place.

> *The Brigand of Kandahar* (1965) In 1850 a civilian escort party leaves Fort Kandahar on the North-West Frontier of India. Unbeknown to them, they are going to be ambushed by the villain, the Brigand himself. They ride out on horseback through a clearing, in front of the fort (though in reality this is just a rather crude painting standing on a large rock at the back of the

set). Then they pass a gigantic cliff-face to their left. Later on, they hit the same clearing again. Everything is more or less the same, except that the fort is now further away – a smaller painting, but standing on the same rock at the back of the set, which is partially hidden by a small bush. Then they pass a gigantic cliff-face to their left. Later still, they draw to a halt in a clearing, or rather *the* clearing and are ambushed. The fort is so far behind them now that it cannot be seen at all, although the rock it was standing on is still there, the same size, at the back of the set. This time round, the cliff-face has a deep recess in it and conceals the Brigand's secret mountain hideaway.

Warning Two: Whichever means of transport they choose to go on, make sure that when they set off, it goes with them.

Arabian Adventure (1979) A magic carpet is unrolled and spread out on the ground. Two people climb on to it with baskets of fruit. The carpet stiffens to take their weight and then flies away. This is a special effect! Ingeniously done by bringing in another, stronger carpet in between shots, one that will take the actors' weight as it moves. Unfortunately, after they have flown off, the old carpet that they laid down originally is still there where they left it. You can tell, because one man catches his foot on it and kicks it up into shot.

And lastly three: Make sure when the characters set off from a place, that they leave the place behind them.

The Terrornauts (1967) A space-craft, standing on an asteroid in outer space, has a view of its rocky terrain out of the window. Yet, when they take off and fly away, while they are travelling the surface of the asteroid stays with them outside the window.

Fire Maidens From Outer Space (1956) After the rocket to Jupiter is launched and the crew are cruising through space, you can hear the sound of heavy traffic passing by outside!

Flashback Country

Flashback Country

As audiences go, schmovie-buffs are a pushy and inquisitive lot. Before we can really settle down to pick holes in a picture, there are certain facts we insist on knowing – the end, for a start. Most people want to know how a film will end, but are quite content to wait until they get there to find out. Not us. By that time, as you'll see, it may be too late. We want this information well in advance. To spot mis-takes properly, it is helpful if we can discover right at the beginning the direction a story is going to take, which of the characters will be lovers, which of them are cheats or heroes or double-dealers; who will die halfway through, and so on – if only to release us from having to follow the plot too closely while we're out fishing for goofs.

Fortunately, in many schmovies most of these details are dropped deliberately into the storyline like dead weights early on – usually in the first 15 minutes – equipping you with all the facts you will need to know in one cumbersome dollop.

For instance, keep a close watch on the old man in disaster movies, who mentions in passing, when we meet him initially, that he was once a key member of the Belgrano Brothers highwire act until he lost his nerve, and mark it well, because towards the end, when this guy and his wife are trapped alone on the roof of a burning skyscraper, and when the sole way to fetch help is for *someone* to walk 200 yards across a thin steel cable to the neighbouring building, he will miraculously come into his own. 'I'll go,' he'll say, chalking his feet and leaping to the cable with his arms outstretched, having suddenly regained his pluck.

And that is what we call a plot device: a seed planted in that first quarter of an hour, which can be harvested later on before they reach the closing credits. You could almost put money on it!

'But Johnnie. . .I can't swim!' is another. Anyone who chances to slip this into the conversation will sooner or later find himself diving into rapids off a 60-foot ledge, or thrashing helplessly about in the foam after a shipwreck. You can see it coming. Nobody prepared to admit to any sort of incapacity in films can do so without suffering for it in due course. Phobias and infirmities are milked for all they are worth. Dizziness, black-outs, heart trouble, you name it – each will be fully exploited before the picture is through. Asthma sufferers are an absolute menace for this. When a character announces he is asthmatic he is telling you two things: one, that he has asthma, and two, that he will have one of his attacks at the worst possible moment – during a siege maybe, or while he is stuck in a crowded elevator between floors, or as the jet-engines on an aeroplane cut out and it starts to bank over and descend rapidly. Only then will he slump into a corner, clutching at his collar and wrestling to pull the cap off his inhaler.

Because time is short, a writer daren't waste a split-second of it telling you something you do not need to know, which makes the task of writing rubbish a tough one; tougher, in some cases, than writing quality stuff.

Pity, then, the frustrated schmovie-author sitting at his typewriter at 4.30 in the morning with an ugly 10 o'clock deadline to beat. Waist-deep in waste-paper after trying to work the same set of facts into the first scene in 400 different ways, and down to his last Mogadon, he has slipped into the sort of trance that comes from staring at an empty vodka bottle for too long. The whole situation can lead him into very serious temptation. The urge is soon upon him to unlock his desk and pull out that battered copy of the Cliché Code he keeps there for emergencies. He knows full well that inside it he will find a wealth of answers to his problems – a list of Ten Little Helpers that the struggling idea-less writer may recruit at any time to assist him in carrying his story forward; tips on how to alter the texture of his script for effect, how other authors before him have coped with the problems facing him right now, and, maybe most importantly, how best to cram his plot devices into the opening 15 minutes of the film: little touches that, if applied diligently, are sure to make his movie no different from anyone else's.

Sadly, it is a temptation that few are able to resist – even expert scriptwriters succumb occasionally.

The Ten Little Helpers are as old as the hills, each one wearing thin after constant use, but none of them any the less popular for that. Again, it feeds on examples drawn from half a century of popular film-making.

Little Helper Number One: The Letter

No one in a film who opens a letter or finds a message left pinned to his bedroom mirror is able to keep the content of it to himself for very long. He automatically assumes we want to know what it says. Just as well he does, too, because a lot of basic plot information can be passed on in letters, telegrams, ransom demands and goodbye notes – 'Dearest Kip, I have gone. Please do not come after me. We shall never meet again, my love. You see, I have found another. It is much bigger than the first. Thank you for everything. Affectionately, Isabel.'

Either the message will be held up to the camera, probably with the vital part illuminated to catch our eye, in which case it must be typed, or written in clear, bold, together handwriting. (People with squiggly, illegible, untogether handwriting never have a letter of theirs held up to the camera.) Or, and this is more popular, it will be read aloud to us. The recipient may read it himself, first of all, or he may pass it on to someone else, making a weak excuse: 'I can't read without my glasses. Will you read it to me?' *(The Way to the Stars,* 1945); 'I can't read it. I'm too nervous.' *(Little Women,* 1949); or, equally, he may imagine that the voice of whoever wrote it is reading it to him.

Take care with this last one. If you do hear the voice of the author, make sure that what he says is what is actually written on the paper.

> *The Bermuda Triangle* (1978) An astronomer receives a letter from a fellow scientist. 'My dear Jessop' – the sender's voice – 'in our responsibility to science, can we forget our humanity?' But if you pay close attention to the page being held up to the camera, what that sentence really says is, 'Anyway, I think this is an interesting angle worth. . .experimentation, do you?'

Little Helper Number Two: The Flashback

Flashbacks enjoyed the greatest popularity back in the 1960s when it was all the rage to make those stern but colourful adaptations of H.G.Wells' and Jules Verne's classic science-fantasy novels – *The Time Machine, 20,000 Leagues*. . . you know the sort of thing.

Out of the relatively small batch that were made about that time, a 'best way' of introducing the story evolved, and has been taken up in many other films and television series since. The picture should open in a country nursing home. An elderly explorer sits smothered in blankets and padlocked to a wheelchair, from where he recounts to a gawping reporter the fantastic adventure he had when he 'accidentally went to the Moon', or when his diving bell slipped through a fissure in some ocean trench or other, and he discovered a lost civilization, the remains of Atlantis, or Captain Nemo, presumed dead but still alive and working.

'It all began in the year of our Lord eighteen hundred and ninety-three – June the 24th. I found a curious note stuck to the door of my carriage. At first I paid it little heed, but subsequent events soon conspired to change my mind. . .' Then comes the flashback. Present action merges with the past by way of a queazy-ripple effect, as though a stage-hand is standing out of shot tipping honey down the screen. (A similar effect can be achieved at home, if you wear a pair of goggles in the shower. Try it.)

The ripple transports us back 40 years, and only now do we find out why we were introduced to this old windbag in the first place – so that he can spend the rest of the film rambling on and on about his bloody expedition. We get to see the Moon, the civilization, Captain Nemo, Atlantis, and then, after 90 minutes, more honey is tipped down the screen, bringing us quickly to the present again, as he tails off with, 'So you see, young man, there are worlds other than our own. . .worlds we can reach if we only hhhhhh. . .' Then he dies.

The same actor plays both roles – the youthful as well as the demented professor. All make-up artists have their own 'senile old git' kit and, in a couple of hours, a young actor can be given the white, wispy toupée, stick-on silver eyebrows, latex wrinkles and cysts that have come to be the trademark of old age in the movies.

Flashbacks will rarely creep up on you by surprise, you'll find. They are usually well-signposted in the story. The three standard lead-in lines to listen out for are:

1. '. . .it happened on Tuesday. . .I was on my way to the office as usual. . .when. . .' and the scene switches swiftly to the Houses of Parliament with Big Ben chiming the quarter-hour *(School for Scoundrels,* 1960). This one is reserved for the retelling of a joky tale, or for the evidence given by a murder-witness.

2. 'Where did it all begin? I suppose it was when I was at school. . .' *(Curse of Frankenstein,* 1957) – kept for mental patients under psychiatric examination, or prisoners on the night before their execution.

3. 'As long as I live, no matter how far I go from the scene, I shall never forget how it all began. . .' *(Moss Rose,* 1947). A sure indication that whoever can't forget whatever it is, is determined that we won't forget it either. These films usually open halfway through the story, or even at the end, so that by the time you drop in on the characters, hearts have been broken, families wrenched apart, lives lost or shattered, leaving nothing but despair. A house so run-down that water drips relentlessly on to the bed; Papa sits alone in a wicker chair, saying nothing; Momma cries quietly into her dish-flannel; Carol has a leg missing, and gazes broodily into the fire. Something privately cataclysmic has happened to these sorrowful souls, but what? Admittedly, you are *slightly* intrigued as to how they came to be in such a state, but not overly so – not to the extent that you want to sit in an uncomfortable seat for two hours to find out. However, just as you're feeling relieved that all the misery is behind you, and that from now on their plight can only improve, up comes a flashback, dragging you into the past again, and you have to endure the whole history of their torment right from the beginning.

Little Helpers Numbers Three and Four: Narration and the Caption

Linked because they amount in essence to the same thing, these two are the simplest devices at a writer's disposal, and the most boring, too, in many ways, so I shall dispose of them fairly quickly myself.

They are used largely as scene-setters. A caption will tell you in which country or city a film is set. The usual stock-shot Eiffel Tower at the opening of the picture is not enough for some. The Dimwit Element tend to require a caption that says 'Paris', before they can fully grasp what they're being told. 'Paris 1914', superimposed over a panorama of the city rooftops, is even better for us, especially if the film was made entirely in the studio in England or America (as is invariably so when you see a caption like this), since, first, it lets us know that this is going to be a period picture, which is Good News, and, second, it acts as our cue to be on the look-out for TV aerials, fast-moving commuter traffic and Boots le Chemists signs.

Narration, for its part, is little more than a caption read aloud. The best you can do as a schmovie-buff is ensure that what the narrator tells you agrees with what you can see on the screen.

> *The Bermuda Triangle* (1978) A formation of American P51 Mustangs locates a UFO in the skies over Kentucky. Their flight leader, Captain Mantel, radios in to Godman Tower at Fort Knox to report the sighting – message timed at 3pm according to a clock on the wall. After which, the narrator blurts out, 'Then at 2.45, Mantel contacted the Tower. . .'

Little Helper Number Five: Time

Time oils the cogs of a film. Skilfully manipulated, a story can span several decades, if necessary. The writer may shift the action from day to day in his script, or from millennium to millennium. Characters can grow old and die, new generations spring up, poor men become rich and rich men tumble, all in three reels. This capacity to dodge carefreely between centuries and seasons, to hop from here to there without restraint, is the writer's joy. To see his efforts grind inadvertently on to the rocks and break up is the schmovie-goer's joy. A discrepancy may be measured in many ways. It could take minutes . . .

Kiss Me Deadly (1955) Mike Hammer (Ralph Meeker) passes a street-vendor, buys some popcorn off him and walks away with it – a brief sequence lasting nine seconds – if that. Yet, watching the clock in the window behind him, you'll see that he walks up to the vendor at 2.10pm, buys the popcorn at 2.15, and carries on up the street immediately – at 2.20!

The Master of Ballantrae (1953) At the point where Errol Flynn is having an argument with his brother in the film, the candle on the table *grows* four inches while they shout at each other.

. . .or hours. . .

The Corn Is Green (1945) Prim schoolma'am Bette Davis arrives in a Welsh village with her housemaid. When the maid walks in through the door of their new home, the time on the grandfather clock is 12.10. She announces to the people waiting inside that Miss Davis is following right behind and, sure enough, five minutes later, the lady herself strides in through the door – at 5.15, according to the same clock.

. . .or months. . .

On the Fiddle (1961) Staff Sergeant Graham Stark has been keeping a full dossier on a couple of new recruits at an Air Force base. Having earmarked them as loafers, his file maps out their doings and whereabouts 'since they joined us in October. . .' that is, October 1944. But earlier in the film, when we see the two of them signing up to join the RAF, the calendar on the wall says '5th April'.

Jaws (1975) The Amity Swimming Regatta on 4 July is terrorized by a great white shark, which scares most of the holiday-makers off the beach, and all the leaves off the trees as well. The shark scenes were filmed in the spring, the rest of it during the summer, and when the two sets of shots are joined up, the effect is quite jarring.

By far the most vulnerable time for mis-takes to happen is between day and night. For a writer to set a scene at night is one thing, but for his instructions to be translated on to the screen is another entirely.

For Your Eyes Only (1981) Roger Moore is exploring an old warehouse in Corfu after dark when it explodes. The man who set the charges makes a swift getaway by car and speeds off into the night. Moore takes a short cut to head him off: he climbs a flight of steps, runs along a tunnel, up another flight of steps, and then another, and finally reaches the top of the hill before the car does, by which time – ta-raaaaa! – it's daylight and the sun is shining!

A night scene may be created quite easily in the controlled conditions of the studio, as the lights can be dimmed on demand. But studio night is not without its own little problems.

Carry on Spying (1964) Three British secret agents interrogate a stabbed enemy spy under the beam of a hand-held torch. The man dies before he can tell them anything, so they stand up and go – taking the torch with them, but leaving the beam behind.

Spooks Run Wild (1941) A young girl with a torch in her hand stands so close to the man in front of her that the beam casts a small circle of light on to his shirt. Yet, rather curiously, the beam that came into the room when she walked in carrying the torch, is still bobbing merrily away on the back wall of the set, all on its own.

The glow from a battery-operated torch or a lantern is rarely strong enough to light up the whole room in a film. It needs to be boosted by an extra light, shone from behind the camera and moved, as required, to correspond with the movement of the one in shot. Sad to say, this normally works quite well. But when you are checking these things, don't forget to make sure that there is one beam *per* lamp.

Blood From the Mummy's Tomb (1971) An archaeology expedition penetrates deep into an unlit Egyptian tomb. The members of the team file through the door, each with his own lantern, but apparently sharing one 'glow' between them. The guy standing at the back of the camera with his booster-light trains it on one man at a time, keeping it there long enough for him to scramble into the chamber, before bouncing it on to the next lantern, leaving the first guy stumbling around in the dark.

At times, shadows and silhouettes can be more trouble than they are worth, too.

> *Circus of Horrors* (1960) One of the circus performers eavesdrops on a conversation going on in a sideshow tent by hiding behind a notice-board outside. From where she is standing, she casts a clear shadow across the canvas wall of the tent. But when you see her silhouette from inside the tent, it is of her only – no notice-board.

> *The Intelligence Men* (1965) During a performance of *Swan Lake* by a Russian ballet troupe, members of the cast are being knocked off by a mystery killer. His next victim is the lead male dancer in his dressing-room. When the door is pushed open, the dancer is out of sight, sitting at a table around the corner, shaving. All we can see is his shadow against the back wall. The killer takes his gun by the butt, creeps up behind the dancer and slugs him over the head. But look closer. Before the attack, when the door swings back, the killer's shadow is already in the room! It is standing to one side, waiting for the man to pass through the door. Once he is out of the way, the shadow takes over and does the rest.

If it ever happens that they have to film a night-time sequence, but they wish to do it during the day, then they do it by hanging a special filter over the lens – enough to subdue the sunshine, darken the picture overall, and so give a rough impression of gloom. The filter only tends to work on overcast days, when there are no obvious shadows. If it is done in bright sunshine, it merely throws a thick blue fug across the picture, and creates much the same effect as when you hold a boiled-sweet wrapper up to your eye. They keep on telling you it's midnight, when you can see for yourself that it is mid-afternoon. They think we're fooled, they think we don't notice. But we're not and we do.

The lousy blue fug effect is known to schmovie-goers as 'broad daynight', and accounts for many a strange hiccup. It explains how Dracula, who only moves about at night, can be found wandering through a wood in the daytime, apparently unbothered by the sunshine *(Dracula Has Risen From the Grave,* 1968); and how a young girl can leave her bedroom at the dead of night, run off into the local village seemingly on a sunny day, then reach the vicar's house two minutes later at the dead of night again *(Captain Clegg,* 1962); and how a secret agent can break into a prison building at night, and burst out five minutes after in brilliant sunlight *(Jaguar Lives,* 1979).

In many cases, they try to pass the effect off as very, very strong moonlight, just like they used to do in Westerns 40 years ago. The sort of very, very strong moonlight that makes you screw up your eyes at the glare, that sparkles on water *(Vera Cruz,* 1953) and glints fiercely off anything metallic *(Sea of Sand,* 1958).

In *Jaguar Lives,* it looks as though they didn't bother using a filter at all. And they certainly didn't in:

> *The Wonderful World of the Brothers Grimm* (1962) In the fairy-tale episode about the princess and the woodman, the king hires a happy-go-lucky woodcutter to find out where his daughter goes to at night, and how she manages to wear holes in her shoes. As it turns out, when the princess leaves the palace on these nocturnal jaunts, she merely pops down to the forest to groove with the gypsies, toe-heeling around their camp through the small hours and returning before dawn. The thing you will notice is that it is as bright and sunny when she sneaks away at midnight, as it is when she gets back in the morning.

Little Helper Number Six: Language

As a rule, audiences in western cinemas do not warm to films in which the actors speak an alien language. Pictures in Hindustani or any one of the 200 Cameroonic dialects, or French, may be all-time blockbusters back home, but will not be terribly popular where it matters most – in the West, which you can take in this context to mean west of the English Channel.

To be a widespread success, a film must be understood in Britain and America without subtitles or dubbed voices being added: subtitles because they are such an inconvenience – reading them while you follow the story is rather like trying to dig the garden and retile the roof at the same time; whereas dubbed dialogue, even when it is done well, makes for an infuriating distraction, since the voices never tie in exactly, or even remotely, with the mouth movements. This was proved over and over again in pictures such as *Godzilla Versus the Smog Monster, Tidal Wave, Matango, Fungus of Terror,* and dozens of other cinematic suppositories inserted into our culture in the 1960s by the Japanese film industry, in which a four-minute monologue spoken with passion and conviction and urgency would be interpreted simply by the one caption: 'Come on – let's go!'

So if a scene is set in distant parts, and foreign tongues are involved, the writer must somehow twist the conversation round and introduce into it a good excuse for everyone to abandon their own language and speak ours instead.

Red Planet Mars (1952) The Martians have somehow come by a copy of the New Testament and are sending religious messages to Earth, causing alarm among the Super Powers, not least in the Soviet Union where top level talks at the Kremlin are continually drowned by communal hymn-singing from the streets, as Communist chants and slogans are quickly ditched in favour of a Thanksgiving Day knees-up. Inside a committee room, as one chap is making a crucial point to his comrades in Russian, the chairman stops him abruptly. 'Speak English – fool!' After which, everyone in the room speaks English, for no reason I could readily discern, save that if they hadn't, the whole point of the scene would have been lost on us.

The Half-Breed (1952) An Indian squaw runs to her brother, babbling in their native tongue: 'Shickoshen yor-ash tahayo. . .' she pleads, which I roughly translate as, 'Quick, do something! Nobody understands a word I'm saying!' To this he replies in a flash, 'When you speak to me, little sister, try to speak in English – then you know *two* proud languages.' Brilliant! Pure mastery of the technique.

Little Helper Number Seven: The Journalist

Since an audience usually joins a story when it is partly over, in that we enter people's lives having missed everything that has happened to them before we paid our money and sat down, the things we ought to know have to be explained to us in full so that the story can develop from there. They could, if they chose to, let you try and work it out for yourself. But we can't be left in the dark for too long in the vague hope that we'd deduce it all for ourselves. Also, they have the Dimwit Element to consider again here. It would only take one of *them* to lose the thread, to tell his friends that the film is a muddle and not worth seeing, and soon everybody would be staying at home. This is too great a risk for a director to take, and therefore everything that is important is said clearly, out loud, at length, in earshot and, to this end, characters quite often go out of their way to give each other information of which they are already fully aware.

The Guns of Navarone (1961) Anthony Quayle tells Gregory Peck, 'Before the war you were the greatest mountain-climber in the world.' Something that Peck knows already, of course, and doesn't need to be reminded of, though we do. Since they are about to embark on an impossible climbing mission, this fairly major point needs to be cleared up before they start.

The Battle of the Bulge (1965) Colonel Hessler (Robert Shaw) has the full Nazi air-attack capacity of V1s and V2s explained to him in considerable detail, with models and visual aids, even though he is a high-ranking German officer to whom all of this must surely be old ground. But in the circumstances, he suffers in silence for our benefit, in order that we can learn how lethal the German arsenal is.

These are essentially one-off examples. The task of reminding us of the story-so-far is usually left to journalists. Any obscure plot-detail or matters of background can be sorted out in no time at all, by letting the leading characters cross the path of a reporter before the story starts in earnest.

Torn Curtain (1966) Paul Newman is a physicist who appears to be defecting from the West with his latest invention. He arrives in East Berlin under escort, to face a pack of wild journalists. 'Sir,' begins one of them, 'is it true you're defecting because Washington abandoned your anti-missile project?' Not bad as an opening thrust. Neat, well-written and concise. 'Professor,' a second hack says, 'is that the anti-missile missile? The one that's supposed to make nuclear defence obsolete?' Needless to say, it is. Ten minutes of exposition condensed into 25 seconds. And now you know everyth. . . 'Does that mean. . .?' A *third?* '. . .that you plan to hand over your secret to a Communist country?'

Yes, yes, yes! This device will carry on indefinitely and take over if something isn't done to put an end to it. So usually the interviewee will wind up by being bundled into a waiting car. Either that, or an official will step in from the sidelines and usher the journalists away with 'That's enough. . .no more questions,' which means they've told us all we need to know for the moment, and isn't it about time we got on with the goddamned story?

Little Helper Number Eight: The Stock Character

Once a director has fully identified his principal characters, and worked on their backgrounds, attitudes and behaviour, he must then turn to consider the peripheral roles – barmaids, waiters, postmen, whoever, satellites orbiting around the central figures, whose personalities and histories need only a light dusting of detail – nothing too specific. This is where the Cliché Code comes in very handy, by providing both writer and director with a range of ready 'stock' characters which an audience will have seen 100 times before in other films and will therefore recognize instantly.

Regular appearances over the years have invested these people with a number of well-established characteristics and mannerisms. So stock drunks behave the way stock drunks behaved in other pictures, stock doctors behave like other stock doctors, stock farmers like stock farmers, and the same goes for any of the hundreds of other screen stereotypes, from whores to shop-assistants, gay hairdressers to crotchety aunts, ageing manservants right through to frightened Malaysian guides on lost river expeditions. You can picture for yourself, approximately, what any one of them looks like, and how they might walk and speak, long before they ever appear on the screen. Their backgrounds are filled in effortlessly using the viewer's own memory and imagination.

This makes sound sense. Why should a director be original and fritter away precious dialogue explaining who some new characters are and what they are like when he can take these neatly-rounded people 'off-the-peg', and kill two clichés with one stone?

To get you started with stock characters, I have picked out three from the many listed in the Code as a taste of what you can expect.

The Stock Biddy

Wherever this woman goes in films, disaster erupts in her wake. Once she decides to board a ship, then you know that the voyage is doomed. It could capsize, strike an iceberg, spring a leak, ram a trawler or have a homicidal maniac somewhere on the upper deck. If you find her strapping herself into a seat on an aircraft then, sure as anything, the whole flight will be marked by incident – either the plane will develop engine trouble and be forced to put down on water, or it will plunge out of the sky into a mountainside. But you'll also find her at the head of a queue in a bank, making a complaint just before an armed robbery that leaves 70 per cent of the customers and staff dead, and the rest held hostage; or walking her hairless chihuahuas down Rodeo Drive when her bag is snatched. What's more, she's even worse than an asthmatic in any kind of siege.

Likely as not, all the script called for was 'an old lady', with no further qualifying remarks. But the experienced director knows what it means and immediately he will invoice the casting agent for a 'stock biddy', a lively, chuckling widow, cute, irresistibly lovable, neatly dressed, freshly washed and powdered, with her hair thrown up into a bob and a square of cream lace at her cuff, ready to pull out whenever she gets round – as she surely will, believe me – to relating brief episodes from her normally quite horrific past to the 'young man' in the next seat: her first husband drowned in a freak white-water rafting accident in Vermont; or her only daughter was brutally slaughtered by Bedouin tribesmen on her honeymoon – that kind of thing. It follows the same routine every time – first the memories, then the sniffles, then the handkerchief, then the distress and horror, but she does it with such well-practised ease and a charm that is sweet enough to sicken.

This is strictly Tinseltown senility, you understand, perpetuated by too many cosy television commercials portraying old age as fun, the way it ought to be – carefree, warm, comfortable and healthy to the last gasp. Nothing like reality, in fact. No mention of inflamed joints or wet patches on sheets, or special walking frames or 'homes'; and so far removed from all those ga-ga grannies with buckled spines and shabby overcoats who sit with their legs wide open in supermarket doorways, talking to their groceries and smelling like a stevedore's vest.

The Brains-in-Her-Bristols Blonde

A standard feature of those swinging comedies and cheap, seedy thrillers produced in the sixties, the era in film history when the cinema first became chest-conscious, was the Brains-in-Her-Bristols Blonde.

There was never any more to her than met the eye; her intelligence was minimal, though I don't doubt that she had more than the producer who hired her to play in his films. Rather, what she had was immaculate lacquered hair – a tribute to the topiarist's art – held back with a wide white headband, full lips, shiny, red and fixed permanently into a half-pout; smoothly-tapered sapling legs; generous hips packed into a mini-skirt three sizes too small, with just a smile of buttock peeking out from underneath; and, of course, the boobs, the giant boobs, apportioned so that they fell in perfect symmetry. She was supposed to represent Mr Average's idea of Miss Wonderful, his unattainable dream-girl, but when these films are re-run on television today, all of a sudden she looks so terribly plain.

The B-I-B Blonde is possibly the least amusing and most offensive of all the stock characters. What makes it worse is that she never died out; the girl is still around today, still unable to act, but nevertheless taking that first step in the profession using her figure as a passport to a big break. For her, success is just a matter of being in the right bed at the right time. To land the part and to catch the producer's eye, she has done everything the agency told her to do: She has Ryvita'd her body, Slimcea'd it, Nivea'd it and Jane Fonda'd it until her waist is within a hair's breadth of being. . .well, a hair's breadth. It may have been acceptable in the sixties. Now, it's humiliating and sad.

If you discount the current rash of successful High School 'growing up and doing it for the first time' movies, the B-I-B blonde turns up in seven clearly-definable situations:

1. The stereotypist: the vain and fabulously-titted personal secretary. Bearing a tray of coffee or a sheaf of papers, she teeters into the office on impossible heels, teeth, hair, hips, lips and chest, all in synch, the lines she has been given to say – 'Here's the Feldman Contract you asked for, Jeff' – obviously playing on her mind. When the words actually arrive, each syllable screams, 'Hey, look, everybody, I'm *acting!'* After a glorious 55 seconds in shot, she edges out again, but slowly – careful not to snag her breasts on the door knob as she leaves, pulling the door to behind her, never to be heard of again.

2. The busty hitchhiker in the bright red hugger shorts, found tinkering cluelessly under the bonnet of her car at the roadside, waiting for a man, such as Leslie Phillips, Kenneth Connor or any one of the other faded British comedy actors with well-practised leers, to stop by and help her – and note, it is always a man who stops, never a woman.

3. The attractive girlie motorist sitting at the traffic lights in her open-topped Spitfire, applying lipstick or eye-shadow in the rear-view mirror, to the gloating delight of the lorry driver in the next lane. In this situation, the cameraman rarely misses an opportunity to high-dive into her cleavage with his lens.

4. Anyone to this day who surveys the view through a telescope or binoculars will find one of these girls undressing in her bedroom, or easing out of the bath, unaware she is being spied on.

5. Whenever a man has to climb out of his hotel window, inch along the ledge outside and climb in through the window of the room next door, he always stumbles upon one of these girls, standing half-naked, clipping on her bra, or in bed with her lover. All she has to do

for this is sit with her mouth open and pull the duvet up over her acting ability.

6. She is one of the first people to be invited to one of Leo's far-out opium parties, and spends the whole evening twisting to old Johnny Dankworth EPs.

7. Big-budget spy films are full of B-I-B blondes, though, strangely, she need not be blonde – this is merely a tag of convenience, and it is the mammarial complement that counts, not the shade of dye she has dipped her hair in. B-I-Bs stroll around laboratories in white coats, gripping a clipboard, twiddling knobs knowingly, peering into blinking monitor screens and making note of what they see. The most despicably evil villains seem to employ a steady turnover of these girls in their homes and missile bases. The film's publicity usually calls them 'a bevy of beauties', but they can't hoodwink us with hype. We know who they really are.

The Stock Scientist

It is not enough for a cinema audience merely to be told that a man is a scientist, or so runs the reasoning; nobody is going to believe he truly is one unless he goes out of his way to prove it, by making pointed remarks, dropping king-sized hints and ramming the point home at every available opportunity. On this score, film-makers see you, the viewer, as a cynical, unyielding adversary. They figure that no matter what lengths they go to to persuade you otherwise, you will still be sitting out there in the darkness, staring at the screen and muttering, 'I'm sure that guy's not *really* a scientist!'

But with audience opinion weighted against them, and the battle as good as lost before it's begun, do film-makers give up? Not a bit of it. Instead, they simply double their efforts: they include remarks that are even more pointed than normal, drop bigger and bigger hints, and ultimately call upon a well-established three-phase plan, set out in full in the Code, which answers the question, 'Is there a doctor in the script?'

Phase One: Dress

You can tell a lot about a doctor by the way he dresses.

1. A white-coat-and-spectacles image means reliable, it means informed, an all-round serious thinker who can be trusted to impart the very gravest news at any time – a vital member of the cast may have slipped into a coma (her saline drip came unplugged in the night); he is going to have to operate; the baby is hideously deformed, may

even be a mutant. He walks as he talks, taking off his glasses and slipping them into his top pocket, stopping and turning now and then to pose for a close-up shot when the news gets worse – 'There's no hope. I'm sorry.' 'Only one chance in a million that he'll survive. It doesn't look good.' 'She may never regain consciousness. I'm sorry.' He's always sorry, but can never do anything to help.

On the other hand, it is quite rare for a patient to die if the doctor treating him is carrying a clipboard. A clipboard says 'progress', it indicates reassuring news, a change for the better, the possibility of complete recovery, although there are two important exceptions to this. The first is when the doctor is a woman.

Stock characters are only useful so long as the audience recognizes them immediately for what they are. You have to remember that well into the 1950s, many women were being tied to sofas, and were still tripping, falling and getting rescued for a living. To the movie industry, women were always housewives first, glamour-pusses second, plates of meat third, and women a poor fourth – purely functional items, cast to play the love interest rather than the principal character. Girls were made to love and kiss, and that was about it. So this is why, when a space mission needed a touch of romance, and a woman, however regrettably, had to be cast as an astronaut or explorer, she seemed to fit her duties at mission control in between doing the shopping and dusting the house.

> *War of the Satellites* (1958) Only half an hour before the latest satellite is due to be launched to the Spiral Nebular Gann, the one female member of the crew, Sybil, is still at home, putting her coat on and chatting socially to a friend on the telephone.

For these reasons, among others, women have lost a lot of ground over the years, and cannot be taken seriously as doctors on the screen. So to fill the credibility gap in the viewer's mind, women scientists are not only given the white coat and specs, but a clipboard too. It doesn't make their news any better, it simply means they are more acceptable in the role.

Mind you, if you thought women were badly placed in the cinema's Inconsequentiality League, then you should consider the plight of black people. They are so far down the table that there is nothing below them but horses and cockroaches, and after that you drop off it altogether.

Although they managed to shrug off the zip-a-dee-doo-dah image of broad-beaming 'Yus, Masser!' butlers, handymen, cooks and shoeshine boys a long time ago, and although big-name actors such as Richard Pryor and Eddie Murphy have made it to the top on pure talent, and in spite of any natural prejudice they may have encountered on the way up, as yet black people do not fit so easily into a film that the whole story can go by without at least some reference being made to their colour. What change there has been, was spearheaded as far back as 1955 by *The Blackboard Jungle*, and then *The Defiant Ones*, *The World, The Flesh and the Devil* and others, when attitudes in films began to reflect social change. As discrimination against blacks became a topical issue, so a small coterie of talented black actors rose to prominence and became much in demand. One apocryphal message from those days, sent by a Hollywood mogul to his casting agent, read:

> I told you on the telephone,
> T'hire me Harry Belafonte;
> If he's busy or away,
> Get me Sidney Poitier!

Even now black actors cannot comfortably be cast as scientists. In schmovie-terms, this means that the credibility gap is practically unbridgeable, and consequently, to be convincing as doctors, they must not only have the standard-issue white coat, the glasses and the clipboard tucked tightly under the arm, but also, to round it off and kill any last nagging worry you may have that they are just pretending, a stethoscope!

A stethoscope, you'll find, is the piece of apparatus carried by any doctor whose identity is in doubt.

2. The second style of dress is the brown tweed suit and crushed plaid fishing hat, worn by ageing country doctors on call, plus a few scatty college professors. From this you can tell he will turn out to be a doddery guessworker. He works purely off hunches, and rants and gibbers breathlessly about things that nobody, not even he, understands. As a doctor, he only ever carries with him the one piece of equipment he is likely to need for the next scene.

> *The Beast From Twenty Thousand Fathoms* (1953) In this, the doctor says, 'Bring me my bag!' When he opens it up, all he has inside is one stethoscope, and nothing else.

His favourite part of any film is when he gets to stand by a bedside, shaking his head as he pulls the sheet up across the patient's face and says, 'There was nothing I could do. I'm sorry.' He is usually a good deal sorrier than the other guy, if only because most of his patients seem to die long before he has finished with them. The knowledge that he is attending to their case seems only to exacerbate the condition. The reason he gets away with it so often is that he treats people quietly at home. The white-coat-and-glasses chap can't do that, because all his patients have to be rushed down hospital corridors on a trolley while they watch the lights flash by on the ceiling above them. This means they are treated much sooner, and therefore survive.

Phase Two: Science

While the clothing they wear is important, that is just the start of it. Once a scientist looks the part, he must next try and convince you that he is qualified to do the job. So with this in mind, the writer tends to throw various dabs of information into the dialogue, a few rogue technical terms and references to vaguely sciencey things that have little bearing on the story, but that are the sort of topics real scientists might refer to in conversation. Isotopes have always been a big favourite here; gravity is another, but also in the running are neutrons, molecules, fall-out, forceps, vortex and the all-purpose scientific fobbing-off term – gamma rays. A bogus scientist will blame everything he can on gamma rays in the confidence that no one watching will know sufficient about them to contradict what he says.

These key words and phrases are traditionally worked into the script by way of a fairly facile conversation held early on, in which he and another similarly sham professor set about telling each other things that, if the pair of them were genuine, they would know anyway. Ideally, this should be conducted against a background that serves to reinforce the overall suspicion you may be harbouring by this time that they *are* scientists, after all: posters of 'The Earth' and 'The Moon' on the wall maybe *(The Terrornauts,* 1967); or a detailed diagram of 'The Human Ear' *(The Curse of Frankenstein,* 1957); or if the set is meant to be a biology lab, there ought to be stacks of wire cages with rats snuffling about inside them, a rather manky-looking spider in a jar, and the now-compulsory human skeleton hanging from a stand in the corner.

Finally, to keep up the pretence, schmovie scientists usually have the most elementary school textbooks littered about their study or office. One laboratory in *The Great Spider Invasion* (1975), has a book carefully placed in shot, entitled *Physics,* while in *The Bermuda Triangle* (1978) an internationally respected astronomer sits over breakfast with a copy of a book called *The Stars* prominently nestling on the table in front of him.

Phase Three: The Disregardables

You'll find there are broadly four types of screen scientist you can happily disregard:

1. Don't put your faith in any scientist (or indeed anyone else, for that matter) who says 'According to my calculations. . .' when there's no possible way he could know what he is about to tell you. It's another

fobbing-off phrase that means that, having no real facts to hand on the subject, they have made some up. And this applies to the doctor or professor who, when asked a question, replies with, 'Oh, that would take far too long to explain.' Or 'Take my word for it – I'm a scientist' or 'Trust me!' Needless to say, you shouldn't.

2. Be especially cautious, too, of any scientist whose laboratory is packed to the walls with first-year chemistry equipment: flasks, tubes, bell-jars, rubber hosing, burners, tripods, pestles, curly pipes and glass beakers filled with gaily-coloured liquids, bubbling erratically and letting off faint wisps of gas. It's all for show and, pound to a penny, he won't know what half of it is for.

3. Beware of the doc-meet! I don't normally use abbreves myself, but this is a fairly well-known piece of schmovie jargon. The doc-meet is a device used by film-makers, as an alternative to the journalist, for relating the story-so-far. It involves a roomful of concerned scientists, each with half-moon spectacles and a clipboard, sitting with their legs crossed, mumbling and nodding knowingly as another concerned scientist, who is just as phoney as they are, addresses them with the most inflammatory wildspeak. 'Gentlemen, there is a crack in the world!' or 'Gentlemen, we have a confirmed sighting of a UFO!' or 'Gentlemen, the world as we know it will cease to exist precisely six days from today!' If the film opens with this kind of assembly, then you may well be heading for a flashback, and the complete set of circumstances leading up to that statement will be shown in full. None of them is to be trusted. All are just performers pretending to be profs, and can once again, be disregarded, as can the last sort.

4. The white-haired genius who seems to be taken along on all voyages to distant uncharted isles, forgotten plateaux or lost worlds inhabited by Stone Age tribes and a number of jerky rubber dinosaurs. This is the man who runs across rhinoceros-sized hornets, or plants that suck his arm in up to the shoulder, and wheezes, 'Most interesting.'

   Permanently out of breath with excitement, he will pick up a peculiar creature that the props department knocked together at short notice the night before out of three grapefruit segments, two cotton-bobbins and a set of joke rubber udders, and will gasp: 'A species of lepimolluscrodipodicus. Fascinating.' Next, he will trip over a bush that shoots poisoned feelers around his ankles and flings him into a lake. After struggling to the surface by catching his umbrella on a well-placed rock, he'll splutter: 'Well, I never! Absolutely fascinating. Wait until the Institute hears about this!' And so it goes on. He tackles all the awaiting perils benignly and methodically, each one more dangerous than the last – and at least one of which is bound to be a fight to the death between two colossal lizards that are really only two tiny lizards magnified with a special lens – and each forgotten the moment it is past, to be replaced by an even greater calamity around the next inlet. 'Fascinating. This is incredible. . .' Ignore this man. He is a nonsense and a trouble-maker.

Little Helper Number Nine: Scene-Setting II

Nothing in film-making is quite so glaring as poverty.

An old schmovie adage you may have heard of comes to mind here: 'Cheapers is as cheapers does', which, essentially, means that if a picture was shot cut-price, then it will almost certainly look cut-price at the cinema when it is released.

The writer may set his script anywhere in the world he chooses, and have consecutive scenes jumping from Hong Kong to the Andes to Venus to Spalding, but when the film goes into production, if the budget is only a modest one, his lavish globe-tripping scenes will need paring down considerably to match the cash available. It may be that the shots they intended to film in the Andes will now have to be completed on a wood, chicken-wire and plaster mountain constructed on the backlot. An old quarry they have found in Kent will double up for the Venutian landscape. For some, even a mock-up mountain and a trip out to a nearby quarry amounts to extravagance bordering on the prodigal. If that is the case, the producer has two facilities he can fall back on – back-projection and glass-painting. Some use them for convenience alone, others because it is dirt-cheap, but both cause innumerable problems I'm pleased to say.

Back-projection

The trick here is to position a screen outside the door or window of a room built on the studio soundstage, and to project on to it from behind an already prepared piece of film, freshly-shot or drawn from the archive, which gives the impression to the audience that the room is not in the studio at all, but right out there on location. It is a neat way of giving your hotel set an authentic-looking view across old Vienna, or Naples or Trinidad, anywhere you fancy, without ever going near the place. Similarly, a train can be made to look as though it is passing through an Alpine meadow; a car can race through New York at top speed as the driver chats lazily to his passenger, without having to watch the road. And so a sequence that could easily have mopped up a large percentage of the budget has been done for peanuts.

Battle Beneath the Earth (1976) Two policemen on patrol in the streets of Las Vegas are passing brightly-lit sonisacs and restaurants selling ekacnaps. It takes a while before you realize why. The film outside the car window is being shown the wrong way round, and everything on it is therefore backwards.

The Love Bug (1968) During a cross-country race Herbie the Volkswagen is misdirected down a road that leads to a mineshaft. As he speeds into the mine the entrance is rectangular, but out of the back window, the entrance receding into the distance behind the car is round.

North by Northwest (1959) Cary Grant and Eva Marie Saint are dining together in the restaurant-car of the 20th Century train, travelling to Chicago. Their romantic conversation is crucial, and to capture it properly, the camera switches back and forth between the two of them as they speak. Outside the window, the countryside is projected on to a screen, run through the projector first of all when the camera is pointing at Grant, and again for the shots of Miss Saint, facing the other way. One can only guess, after all this time, how far they went to synchronize the two. But having seen it, my guess is – not far. To start with, there is a timber-yard over Grant's shoulder, and Miss Saint is passing some woods. After that, Grant hits the same timber-yard a second time, while from Miss Saint's side there's a tram-shed and a pulping mill going by, and she looks as though she may be heading for the woods again. All this, and Grant is still by that timber-yard. After Miss Saint has struggled past the woods this time, you might suppose that Cary Grant would pass them too. But no, he's back at the timber-yard again. In the course of things, I suppose, none of this really matters, but with the flowers on the table wilting and blooming and wilting and blooming in alternate shots as well, it is very hard to concentrate on what the couple are talking about. To this day, I still don't know.

Film-makers encounter most difficulties in this area when they run the same piece of film through the projector for each new shot, in an attempt to synchronize the background. Ultimately, at its worst, this results in identical events recurring a number of times in a matter of seconds, waylaying the eye and distracting the mind.

The Bulldog Breed (1960) Norman Wisdom stands on a beach on his outward-bound course, and the same seagull flies by at exactly the same angle six times.

The Beast From Twenty Thousand Fathoms (1953) A scientist goes down in a diving bell to inspect some undersea canyons where the beast may be hiding. On this occasion, a seagull, with a second one close on its tail, flies past the camera four times.

Mighty Joe Young (1949) As a novelty, to draw in the punters on its opening night, a club called The Golden Safari has wild animals lining the walls in glass cages, and an enormous gorilla on display. A trio of party guests get drunk and slip some liquor to Joe the gorilla, who breaks away and runs rampant through the club. As he swings on to a thatched balcony roof, two men in dinner jackets escape off it down a vine, but four times! In the resulting mayhem, Joe smashes the glass on one of the display cages, and two lions leap through the hole into the crowd. In fact, the same lions leap out through the hole again and again and again and again, five times in all. Watch out for a large piece of glass in the corner that breaks off as they jump over it, then returns to break off afresh the next time they come around.

The Love Bug (1968) The first time Herbie is taken out on the streets of San Francisco by Dean Jones, he is followed by a large white saloon car, and he drives past a blue Volkswagen moving on one side and a red Volkswagen, then a white one, parked on the other side. The second time Herbie is taken out on the streets of San Francisco, later in the picture, he is followed by a large white saloon car, and he drives past a blue Volkswagen moving on one side and a red Volkswagen, then a white one, parked on the other side.

I should add, however, that you don't need to resort to back-projection to invite this sort of trouble. It can easily happen without, as was the case in *Bullitt,* and a sequence that earned the film its reputation as a classic – same car, same city, same year, same problem.

Bullitt (1968) Steve McQueen plays a detective chasing a car full of assassins through the streets of San Francisco. The villains tear down a hill, past a white car pulling out of a sidestreet on the right, and overtake a green Volkswagen. McQueen, in pursuit, also passes the white car pulling out of the sidestreet and overtakes the green Volkswagen. The villains turn left, avoiding a black car coming up the hill the other way, which jolts to a halt to avoid an accident. McQueen has to turn left also to follow them. Then, on a different street altogether, both the villains and McQueen pass the green Volkswagen a second time, plus the white car pulling out of a sidestreet, plus the green Volkswagen a third time. After which McQueen passes the green Volkswagen a fourth time, whilst the villains turn left, avoiding a black car coming up the hill the other way, which jolts to a halt to avoid an accident.

As a schmovie-buff, you should always be looking for the top of the back-projection screen.

The Bulldog Breed (1960) When Norman Wisdom, still on that outward-bound course, falls over the edge of a cliff and hang-dangles perilously from a rope, you can see the edge of the back-projection screen quite clearly across the top of the picture above his head.

Most of the time, you're not likely to see where the screen ends directly, only by reflection, and only, it seems, in the bonnet of a car.

Adam's Rib (1949) New York lawyers Spencer Tracy and Katharine Hepburn are in their car on the way to work, talking at length about. . .about something that I didn't quite catch. I was too preoccupied with where the sky ends above them, as reflected in the car's bonnet at the bottom of the picture, which shows both the top and the sides of the screen.

School for Scoundrels (1960) Same thing, only this time the reflection is in the bonnet of Terry-bloody-Thomas' car, showing up as a thick black line where the sky stops and the studio roof begins.

On the whole, back-projection works well for all vehicles. The effect of travelling is enhanced by positioning someone from the props department outside the car window, waving a tree or a piece of thick card so that it casts passing shadows across the driver's face, and gives the impression of movement. The chap who does this is called The Tree Grip. (In *Taste of Fear,* 1961, the shadow of a telegraph pole is thrown across the actors' faces time after time, but according to the back-projection outside the window, they are driving down a motorway and are not passing any telegraph poles!)

For windows in buildings, back-projected action is only one choice a director has in trying to achieve a convincing view. There are a few others, the most straightforward of which is 'reality'. They can take their cameras to a real room on a real location with a real view.

Quadrophenia (1979) Set in 1964. A teenage boy's bedroom overlooks a busy London railway line, and as he and his mother are arguing about whether he should get out of bed or not, a bright blue and yellow high-speed train streaks past the window, a train that wasn't in service in Britain for another 14 years.

But if they can't go on location and don't want to use back-projection, they have a range of equally fallible alternatives.

A studio-built room often has a bit of foliage outside the window; a couple of potted shrubs will do, plus a vast expanse of blue cloth stretched across the full width of the window, intended to represent the sky. (Watch this! It is not uncommon for actors to walk past a window or door and cast long shadows across a sheet of sky *(Carry on Cleo,* 1964; *Apache,* 1954).

Sets in *really* cheapo films, whose budget won't even run to potted shrubs, will usually settle either for venetian blinds at the window, shut tight so you can't see out, or thick curtains pulled to.

They could use a still-life photograph:

> *The Hunter* (1980) The view from the Sheriff's office in Los Angeles is merely a photo of the city skyline, and you would pay little attention to it were it not for the fact that the building opposite has an air-vent on the roof, emitting a stream of thick white smoke which is completely stationary. Later in the film, we return to the same office when the Sheriff is having a haircut, and the same steam is still there.

They could use a working model:

> *The Blue Max* (1966) The World War I view out of George Peppard's bedroom window is a model, and is supposed to represent an air-raid on German towns on the Western Front. The night sky is lit up, not by explosions, but by two lamps, one on each side of the window, that flash on and off while a string of pretty fairy lights flickers in sequence across the painted hillside beyond, to simulate the ferocity of the attack.

Or they could use a still view:

> *The Little Shop of Horrors* (1960) Outside Mushnik's florist shop is a rather sad street backdrop standing about one and a half inches off the studio floor, and so close to the set itself that pedestrians supposedly walking on opposite sides of the street rub shoulders as they pass.

Glass-painting

Imagine for a moment that a horror-film unit is out shooting the scene where a couple of young newlyweds travel up a mountainside to a deserted monastery to find their missing friend. The location that has been decided upon for the shot is perfect – they have a fabulous, atmospheric mountain, a path winding around the side of it, a forest, a river with a sinister village nestling on its banks – perfect, except for one tiny detail: no monastery. Now, imagine also that they haven't the funds to visit a real European monastery, or to build a scale-model of one back at the studio (from what you have learned so far, this shouldn't take much imagining!) So what can they do? The answer is simple, and above all, cheap.

They lift a sheet of glass into place in front of the camera. A skilled artist then paints the required monastery on to the glass in such a way that when the painting and the landscape are viewed together by the camera, the two images blend into one, and the monastery in the foreground appears to be sitting on top of the mountain in the distance.

Employing the same technique, the four walls of a fake ballroom set can be given a lavish Baroque ceiling with numerous glistening chandeliers; the two thousand Roman tents they couldn't afford can be added to the six or seven that they could; when actors have to inch gingerly along a thin cliff-ledge, with a sheer drop below, that sheer-drop can be painted on glass. A glass-painting can even be used to jolly up a landscape by blotting out some eyesore such as a factory complex or a modern work of art, or putting one in. And provided nobody in the film walks behind the painted portion of the picture, nobody in the audience will be any the wiser.

North by Northwest (1959) After being abducted, Cary Grant is escorted to his car by James Mason's henchmen. The road has been built in the studio, while the hill and the sky behind it are painted on glass. You know this for sure, because one of the henchmen walks too far over in the wrong direction and loses his head completely. It disappears behind the painting.

Day of the Triffids (1962) A whole forestful of hostile plants tries to break through an electric fence surrounding a hacienda in Cadiz. The Triffids nearest the wire are being electrocuted and are giving off sparks, smoke from which vanishes abruptly halfway up the picture – behind the painted Spanish hillside.

Attila the Hun (1954) The smoke from a Hun fire, just before the climactic battle with the Romans, drifts upwards into the air, and eventually slips under a large expanse of painted mountain at the back of the camp.

Taras Bulba (1962) As a test of his manhood, Tony Curtis enters a contest to leap over a steep ravine on horseback. Yul Brynner is officiating. 'Let the will of God be done!' yells Yul, and fires his pistol, causing smoke from the barrel to float slowly across the screen. But instead of going over the ravine as it should do, it disappears *underneath* it. If you have the patience to wait, you will also see it float out again on the other side.

The Terrornauts (1967) An almighty explosion rips through an alien planet. Great grey cauliflowers of smoke fill the air, swirling up and vanishing behind the moon.

Thoroughly Modern Millie (1967) A variation on the theme. Rather than use a glass painting for the scene where James Fox and Julie Andrews are dangling from a ledge on the twentieth floor of an office block, they instead built a mock-up building, or rather part of one, in the studio and merged it on the picture with film of the streets of New York taken from a great height, to make the stunt look even dizzier. And it works well, until Fox leans too far off the ledge and loses part of his head behind the film, and Miss Andrews swings out wildly with her arm and loses it up to the elbow.

Little Helper Number Ten: The Stock Plot

The more films you see the more you come to realize that originality is a commodity in scarce supply, and that those willing to put their money behind something new and different are even scarcer. The dream factory has no time for dreamers any more; foggy-minded accountants and wheeler-dealers are in charge now, looking for safe investments, scrambling to back a possible winner, that is, something that has succeeded many times before and must therefore surely stand another chance this time round, and shying timidly away from the untried and untested.

This in itself is nothing new or different. Writers and directors have always sought to include in their movies elements that went down well in previous ones. After all, that is why the Cliché Code exists – to plug a gap that might otherwise have to be filled by creativity; it is a safety net to ensure a modicum of uniformity and to reassure nervous backers that what worked before for others will work again for them.

When the script is being prepared, therefore, the writer can take out his copy of the Code, flick to the chapter relating specifically to the kind of film he is working on at the time – Western, musical, comedy etc. – and find a ready checklist of elements that he would be well-advised to include.

Let's dip into it ourselves at random – let's take the section on

'Don't-go-near-the-castle. . .' horror-thrillers. To succeed now, a film falling in this category would have to include at least 80 per cent of the following:

Strange goings-on up at the big house, where a crazed genius is conducting bizarre inhuman experiments; a coach that rattles through the forest in broad day-night, taking frightened honeymooners up to the castle, but never bringing anyone back; the coachman who has a broad cockney accent regardless of which country the picture is set in; the horse that rears violently at the sight of a skull on a pole at the crossroads; the dark stranger in a black cape and outrageous wide-brimmed cakestand hat who says, 'Turn back. Leave now, before it's too late!' and who is there one minute and gone the next; lightning storms of a dazzling crash-flash-crash intensity that only seem to happen when travellers are trapped inside a lonely old house on a desolate hilltop, with no transport, in the middle of the night; the gamekeeper found lying in a copse, his throat torn out by some creature too horrible to contemplate (and too expensive to show, probably); the candle-flame that flickers and dies as the French windows burst open in the wind; the constantly-tapping shutters; the leafless tree in the garden that casts peculiarly meaningful shapes across the bedroom wall; the dull thud of a body slumping to the floor upstairs; the restless howling dogs in the grounds.

The shadow of feet outside the bedroom door at midnight; the grandfather clock ticking ominously at the bottom of the stairs; the virgin in a white smock, caught alone in the woods at night when a twig cracks, an owl hoots, and something furry flies out of the undergrowth at her feet; the curious repeated flashing signals from Pug Island out in the bay, where two trawlermen disappeared 'only last week'; strange lights from that room in the attic which was sealed up 20 years ago, about the same time that Her Ladyship went missing; the ever-so-slowly twisting door-handle; the suits of armour on the landing, which move of their own accord (this happens quite regularly, but no one ever explains how they do it); the long staircase with family portraits lining the wall, one of which has two holes cut out of the face and a large pair of bloodshot eyes peering through; the safe behind the tapestry in the study; the swivelling bookcase that opens to reveal a forgotten passageway leading down to the cove; the corpse of a young girl in the drawing-room, which disappears while the person who found it runs off to fetch help – 'But it *was* here, I tell you. I saw it with my own eyes!'; the petrified innkeeper who urges, 'Stay away from the castle. It is a place of unspeakable evil', but who speaks about it to everyone who passes; his beachball-bosomed daughter who collects glasses around the inn and who is usually Dracula's first victim, and his wife called Anna '. . . who cannot forget'; the misty cemetery where all the tombstones are at a slant because they're only polystyrene and someone in the props department thought they looked more mysterious that way; the inebriate gravedigger who runs across a disinterred wolf with a poker through its gullet; the eerie organ music straying from the cellar at all hours; the full moon partly obscured by scudding cloud; the miserable brooding housekeeper with Popeye's face and 'a past' who listens at keyholes; the unjustifiably long oak dining table with ornate candlesticks placed every 200 yards along it; and the deformed butler seen shuffling to the woodshed by night, carrying a head in a bag.

For murder-mystery films, the Code goes one step further by laying down a rigid framework to which all storylines must conform. In the 1950s, when dozens of these pictures were turned out on both sides of the Atlantic as B-features, the Code made it very easy for the writer to produce an acceptable script. With the appropriate plot checklist to hand, he could construct his story systematically, in much the same way as one might knock up a set of kitchen cabinets. Either working alone or in cahoots with others, the whole thing could be thrashed out between gulps of Biryani in a Soho tandoori – a feverish locking-together by committee of all the vital components, one piece at a time, into a cracking tale..

'So this woman in the grey veil is a lady of the night. . .'

'Yeh, and she was murdered by a grotesque figure in a shadowy doorway. . .'

'. . .Ooooh, a stabbing, yes! A vicious bloody stabbing, 71 times in the face and neck – with a jewelled dagger. . .'

(MORE GULPS OF CURRY AS THE PACE HOTS UP)

'And the corpse in the crypt, that was her brother. . .'

'A family cursed by fate. . .'

'Or, even better, the revenge of a madman she once promised to marry. . .'

'A deformed mute. . .'

'No, not a deformed mute. . .a throwback! A throwback who lives in the city sewers and collects things of great beauty.'

'Like jewelled daggers. . .'

'. . .And sells them. . .'

'No, no, and kills ladies of the night, with them. . .'

'Ooooh, another stabbing! He really *hates* those ladies of the night, doesn't he?'

No matter how they develop as stories, it is an established practice that these films should open with a murder, to grab the audience's attention in the first few seconds.

> *The Lodger* (1944) An old woman staggers away from a London pub, waving a beer-bottle which has no label on it. She turns a corner and goes behind a wall, where she is murdered by Jack the Ripper, dropping the bottle on to the pavement, but apparently finding the time to stick a label on it before she dies!

It could equally begin with a headless torso being pulled out of the Thames at Wapping (if the film is set in London, that is; if New York, headless torsos must be fished out of the East River), with one of its hands tattooed 'Green Angel'; the enigmatic lodger found hanging from the light-fitting in his seedy East End bedsit, his pockets jammed tight with used banknotes; the poisoned property heiress on an express train bound for Moscow – anything will do, but the body should always be discovered by a young girl with an innocent face, who pauses for effect, rolls her eyes and screams and screams and screams.

From this point on, the story escapes like a slow puncture, a clue here, a clue there, another few murders, and someone to step in when the plot is at its thickest, to follow up the various leads and to explain the whole conundrum to what is left of the cast after the killer has taken his share of them. There must be a sleuth, and the Code suggests five types:

1. Straight detective work by Inspector Chubb and his junior police sergeant Jenkins is popular; they explain the different elements to each other down at the station, 'You see, it's like a jigsaw, Jenkins, with half the pieces missing.' This was thought to be a terribly astute thing to say in its day, on a par with 'Blackmail's an ugly word, Inspector,' 'You won't take me alive,' and 'I've got a gun and I'm not afraid to use it.'

2. The spunky hack out for a scoop – that old standby the determined journalist again, who by sheer luck happens to be on the spot at the time of the murder and turns investigator. He is usually single, if only because along the way he will find a young unattached, good-looking girl whom he will wish to marry before the credits. The two of them become familiar and fall in love in order to add interest and a bit of urgently-needed sparkle to those uneasy gaps between murders, when the cast are kicking their heels, wondering what to do while they're waiting for the next stiff.

3. The Lone Outsider – the cunning, private superdick from the Hercules Poirot/Sherlock Holmes/Charlie Chan stable, who does things his way, suspecting everyone, and telling them so ('Everyone is a suspect, Madame'), seeing tell-tale signs of guilt in the most inoffensive behaviour, and managing to deduce from the fact that

Lady Hilda took tea on the terrace on Friday afternoon, the day before the murder, rather than on the lawn as usual, that, without a shadow of a doubt, the man from the Post Office 'did it'. He makes irrational guesses, and jumps to conclusions so wild and way-out that only someone who had sat down and studied the script beforehand could possibly follow his line of reasoning.

4. The raunchy, fearless he-man who tracks down the killer seconds before he tries to stab the raunchy, fearless he-man's fiancée, and minutes before the police arrive to arrest him. This is traditionally confined to remote country-house murders, where the body of a millionaire is found at the bottom of a cliff, or at out-of-the-way hospitals where someone has been at the poison cupboard and the staff are being knocked off one at a time. The he-man will assemble the dregs of the cast at the end and say something like 'One of the people in this room is a murderer!'

5. Lastly, the lovable half-cocked spinster, a close relative of the stock old biddy we met earlier, who lives alone in a quiet picturesque Dorsetshire village. Bored out of her tiny cottage, she turns to solving murders, snatching clues out from under the nose of Scotland Yard, always managing to stay one step ahead of the police – an outlandish scenario when you think about it, since the only people one step ahead of the police normally are the criminals.

   It is she who will find the knitting needle with arsenic on the tip in the spaghetti jar, or the bottle of rat-bane concealed in a fold of the bedspread, or the brooch with the bloodstained pin – always taking her lead from a novel she once read, called *Abracadavre* by DeQuincey Marchbank, in which circumstances uncannily similar to those in the present case arose.

> *The Mirror Crack'd* (1980) Miss Marple (Angela Lansbury) sprains her ankle at a garden fête early in the film. From then on, she has to carry a walking-stick – first, in her left hand and then, when her limp inexplicably swaps over to the other leg, in her right hand.

The mystery ends when the killer's identity is revealed. The mask is pulled away and everyone gasps, 'You!', though you can often hardly hear this over the slow-handclapping from the audience, who can barely contain their indifference by this time. The person who committed the murder is always the one person it can't possibly be. It is such a predictable twist now, that the mystery is really no mystery at all – less of a whodunnit, more of a whydeybodderdoinit. 'You!' and it's the chaplain from the local vicarage, or the fresh-faced milkmaid from Hollyhock Farm. 'You!' and the sweet octogenarian widow who teaches religious instruction down at the orphanage turns out to be the brains behind an international kitten-doctoring racket, and on the side has been gunrunning for the Vietcong.

> *Calling Bulldog Drummond* (1951) Drummond is trying to pin down the ringleader of a gang of jewel thieves. The only clue he has to the identity of the Boss is that he has half the index finger on his right hand missing. It is quite a surprise to everyone when Mr Big is found to be none other than Colonel Webson, a fellow member of Drummond's Club and a wealthy socialite. It comes as an even bigger surprise to schmovie-buffs, however, who spotted that in one scene earlier in the picture Webson had all his fingers intact!

INTERMISSION

Putting off the writs

Putting off the Writs

Time now to get down to some serious name-dropping.

We are only part of the way through our quest for kack, but already you may suspect that schmovie-goers are running a bitter and deep-set campaign against certain performers. The same round of names keeps cropping up, with a regularity that smacks of a vendetta.

Perhaps you assumed from what has been said, that by hounding a handful of popular actors – Connery, Astaire, Lancaster, and others – from picture to picture, you had hit on a sure-fire method for uncovering mis-takes; in which case, I had better put you straight here and now. There is nothing personal about schmovie-going, and you will find that steering by the stars leads only to a dead end. After all, to recommend this approach would be as good as saying that any film that contains, for argument's sake, Joan Collins, contains a mis-take as well, which is as good as saying that some films contain mis-takes because they also contain Miss Collins, which is as good as saying she causes them, which is preposterous! We have no actors to grind, please remember that.

If enschmoviasts had to be placed in any category, I would say they were, by nature, pigeon-holers. Where possible, they try to fit an actor into his own little slot, according to the mis-take they know him best for. Once classified in this way, the actor tends to remain in the same slot indefinitely, remembered by Club members for the flaws in his films, rather than for the films themselves, which simply happened to have flaws in them.

Hence, Errol Flynn, for what looks like a minor indiscretion, has been filed away for all time under 'meat'.

> *The Adventures of Robin Hood* (1938) Flynn picks up a large leg of mutton and takes a small bite out of it. Somehow, in one mouthful, he manages to devour the whole joint, and is just left holding the bone.

> *The Master of Ballantrae* (1953) Flynn meets up with an Irishman called Burke, who is eating a chicken. He offers Flynn a wing. Unimpressed, Flynn tosses the wing aside, tears a leg off and hands it to Burke, keep-

ing the rest of the bird for himself. Then the camera-angle changes. Suddenly, Burke is holding the bird, and Flynn has the leg.

For similar petty reasons, Norman Wisdom finds himself under 'buses'.

Press for Time (1966) When Wisdom has his bicycle stolen, he catches a passing bus to chase the thief. The bus is a number 22 when he climbs on board, but soon changes to a number 23, then goes back to being a 22, then to a 23 again, and only returns to being a 22 at the end of the chase when it plunges into the harbour.

Trouble in Store (1953) Wisdom is chasing another bus, this time it's a number 88, across London. First it changes to a number 8, then it loses its number altogether, and finally pulls up as a number 88 again.

Stewart Granger was paid a brief visit by the Goof Fairy in one of his later pictures, and is dearly remembered for this:

The Last Safari (1967) Granger races to help a couple of tourists in Kenya, who are about to be trampled by a stampeding rhino. As he approaches, he is riding in a left-hand drive Jeep. When he arrives, it is right-hand drive.

Then there is Richard Harris:

Camelot (1967) Harris, as King Arthur, goes out into the forest around Camelot to search for Merlin and to spy on Guinevere and Lancelot. It is 500AD, and Arthur has an Elastoplast Airstrip stuck on the back of his neck.

And Joan Collins:

Revenge (1971) Joanie plays the landlady of an English pub, The Crown, whose handpumps clearly are not connected up to anything. To serve a customer with a pint of beer, she has to perform the most elaborate deception. She takes an empty glass, puts it down behind the bar where we can't see it, and pulls the handpump towards her. As she does so, she lets go of the empty glass, picks up an already full one standing by the side of it, and gives that to the customer instead. Though why she didn't simply give him the full one in the first place beats me.

And do note that for cataloguing purposes, it is sufficient that the actor appears in the same film as a mis-take – it does not necessarily have to happen to him.

This Land Is Mine (1943) During a World War II air raid, Charles Laughton makes a dash for cover, taking his old mother with him. She is wearing a hat as she runs towards the shelter but not when she gets there.

Camelot (1967) When Vanessa Redgrave arrives in Camelot at the start of the picture, it is mid-winter and she is wrapped snugly in thick furs against the freezing cold. And yet her little dog, sitting at her side, is panting heavily with his tongue out, under the heat of the studio lights.

At this rate, poor old Peter Finch may only ever be remembered for one film.

The Battle of the River Plate (1956) In 1939, the German Foreign Minister, in tailcoat and top hat, arrives on board the pocket battleship *Graf Spee* in Montevideo Harbour, and is met by Captain Langsdorff, played by Finch. The Minister removes his hat to reveal that he is completely bald underneath, which is an astounding revelation, because as he strolls further along the deck in the very next shot, he has a full head of hair.

But I think every trained spotter goes down on bended knee when you mention the name Burt Lancaster. Doubtless without knowing it, and very likely without much caring either, I should imagine, he has more schmovies to his credit at the present count, than any other living actor.

Soylent Green (1973) Lancaster wears a length of frayed cloth around his neck as a cravat. He pulls it off to take a wash, then turns to face the camera and it is tied around his neck again.

Lawman (1970) In his hotel room, Lancaster takes a shirt off a peg, throws it about his shoulders, and in no time at all, the b. . .oh, sorry. I was forgetting the rules for a moment: no Michael Winner pictures. He directed this one, so I'm going to have to leave you to watch it for yourself. I really do apologize.

Apache (1951) In 1886, on a cold winter's night, Lancaster takes refuge in a barn, making himself comfortable in a horse stall. No sooner has he sat down than the farmer who owns it walks in with a lantern. As he mooches about, nearing the stall where Lancaster is hiding, cast your eyes across to the left of the picture. There you'll find a stage-hand, crouching almost out of sight, behind a small fence. Obviously unaware that filming has begun, he starts unrolling a mattress which springs up out of control and clearly into view–nothing to do with the shot at all. Satisfied that he has ruined the scene completely, he then crawls out on his hands and knees, hoping that we won't spot him.

From Russia With Love (1963) James Bond is in possession of a highly prized coding machine called Lektor, which he is carrying across Yugoslavia in a flower wagon, chased by a helicopter, from which a pair of enemy agents are dropping hand-grenades. One of the grenades hits the wagon bringing it to a halt, blackening the paintwork and blowing out one of its headlamps.

I ought to explain why I have brought this up now of all times. As you may know, Burt Lancaster does not appear in this picture, but he does have the dubious honour of having taken part in a film that contains the most mis-takes in the shortest time. Until that one was discovered, the honour had gone to Sean Connery for *From Russia With Love*.

Bond, wearing a brown Fedora hat, grabs Lektor and makes a run for it. Hiding under some rocks, he shoots down the helicopter, and here come the goofs: a) The moment it hits the ground, Bond's hat disappears off his head; b) He charges back to the flower wagon, carrying Lektor, but arrives without it; c) As the wagon drives off, there are no longer any scorchmarks down the side, and d) The missing headlamp is back in place as well. All four crammed into just 30 seconds of screen-time.

It had to be unbeatable, we thought, but then we hadn't counted on the Daddy of them all:

> *Vera Cruz* (1953) The sequence with the mis-takes in it is at the point in the film we touched on earlier. Gary Cooper and Burt Lancaster are escorting a countess, her carriage and some gold bullion across Mexico. The carriage is ambushed by bandits in a small town en route. Cooper, Lancaster and some soldiers win the day and ride off into the desert. That is the scenario, lasting 90 seconds in the film, yet during that short time, if you are quick, you will see the following: a) The countess's red carriage disappears from beside the wall where they parked it, reappearing again shortly afterwards; b) Burt Lancaster's hat slips off during a scuffle. He stands up and it is back on his head again; c) In the thick of the fight, with soldiers and bandits being slaughtered ruthlessly on all flanks, a small guy is standing off to one side, unbothered by the danger he may be in, leaning against a cart and grinning; d) A dead bandit is lying across a rooftop with no hat on, but when we cut back to him, he's wearing one; e) The shadow of a boom-mike, trying to catch Cooper shouting 'The Carriage!', is cast across the wall of a house; f) Lancaster leaps off Cooper's horse on to a dead soldier lying on the ground, stepping on his head, and squashing it flat; g) A man standing on a haycart in the middle of the street, is shot, and topples to the ground. But when the cart is pulled away, he is still lying on top of it; h) The soldier holding the reins of a covered wagon is shot too. He falls over to one side, and his head drops off; i) A willing peasant girl takes over the reins of the covered wagon and drives it away. By the time it rounds the next bend in the road, someone has fastened the soldier's head back on again; j) The same wagon turns another corner, and now the rest of his body has vanished as well.

Those are the only ones I could find in that 90 seconds. There may be more, I may be mistaken myself, but I don't think so. Check it and see what you come up with.

In spite of all evidence to the contrary, I still maintain that we bear no malice towards the actors we pick on. To us, they are just flickering shapes on a screen, one step removed from reality; and provided they retain the coarsest shreds of professionalism in their work and do their level best, it is hardly for us to question their artistic integrity. I would no more want to say that Britt Ekland can't act for toffee, than I would want her to sue me for saying it – especially since any actress with a reputation worth preserving is apt to stir herself up into a froth over such suggestions, and storm to her lawyers at the first whisper of a slight. For that reason, I'd like to think that our overwhelming urge as schmovie-buffs was to fault the film and leave the actors well alone.

When I am lecturing to converts up and down the country, I lay heavy emphasis on this point, as a reminder to enschmoviasts to have respect for those whose work they are pulling to pieces.

One should never underestimate the amount of drive and stamina it takes for an actor to stay at the top. Lasting popularity is not a chance thing, and must be fought for continually, sometimes at great cost to self. Remaining anonymous is easy – as anyone you've never heard of will tell you, but for those who manage to pull free of the pack and make a name for themselves, the drag back towards oblivion remains strong for as long as they choose to stay in the public eye. An actor is no greater than the sum of his parts, and there can never be any let-up. One slip or misjudgement is all it takes before he is relegated to the bottom of the heap again, scrambling for work, watching his bank balance dwindle, having to move to a smaller house, with only one pool and no sauna, finding himself taken off the 'Homes of the Stars' coach route, and, if things really take a turn for the worst, maybe even having to sign on for a guest spot in an American TV mini-series.

An actor's status is gauged wholly by the media. How and where he ranks alongside his contemporaries at any given time, whether he is 'in' or 'out' professionally, is dictated by radio, television and the press, whose coverage – the amount of attention they give to him, the hoo-hah afforded to his latest project, the number of flash-bulbs flickering at airport arrivals as he pushes through the gate – is the sole litmus of true stardom.

The way an actor is described by the media is a fairly accurate guide to how well-placed he is in the public affection, and over the years, to make the job of classification easier, journalists have devised their own method of grading performers, not just in films, but in the theatre and sport as well, by way of a clever vocabulary of euphemisms which they use to chart their progress. These words and phrases turn up regularly in reviews, newspaper reports, articles, gossip columns, and chat-show introductions, and are taken directly from a checklist incorporated into the Cliché Code, reference to which will tell you at a glance exactly how an actor is doing, whether he is in favour or not – the latest sensation or last week's news. This vocabulary has come to be known as the Success Rainbow.

Reading it off from the lowest end first, it begins with the 'nobody', rising to the 'unknown', then 'young hopeful' – 'newcomer' – 'one to watch' – 'minor celebrity figure' – 'star' – 'big name' – 'superstar' – 'megastar' – 'a man at the peak of his career' – 'legend' – 'stalwart' – 'seasoned entertainer' – 'distinguished figure' – 'master of the art' – 'major celebrity figure' – 'fading light' – 'one-time great' – 'veteran' – 'trooper' – 'has-been', and finally, the saddest of them all, just before they breathe their last and drop off the entertainment twig, 'the grand old man of cinema'.

On the Success Rainbow, as you can see, all the gold is in the middle, and all the old crocks at the end. Looked at this way, the newcomer is simply a has-been in the making, while anyone labelled the grand old man is as good as dead already both professionally and biologically.

Hollywood is a rat-eat-rat world of deals, coups, hype, sensation. It has rarely been anything else, but somehow today it is more cut-throat, more hard-nosed and non-compromising, an altogether more hyphenated town than ever it was. Beverly Hills, its rich suburban satellite, is now a ghetto for yesterday's heroes: people who made their million when they were at the height of their popularity, were subsequently ousted from the limelight to make way for up-and-coming talent, and who would willingly hand over another million to be even half as popular again.

Actresses, once curvy and lithe, their beauty envied the world over, have turned into puddings. Everything they had, everything they were famous for, has sagged and trebled in size. An overdose of the good times – long weekends in Palm Springs, partying till four in the morning, gorging themselves on extravagant five-course lunches, eating everything bar the napkins – has left them lifeless, podgy and old; flesh hangs festooned about their waists in thick pleats and they waddle about the house looking like a sackful of jellies tied at the neck with string. Inside, of course, they are still frisky 20-year-olds, itching to flirt and play as they used to, aching again for the things of youth that deserted them half a century ago. But on the outside, age is corrupting their features. The face is gently crusting over, their complexion taking on a curious open-cast texture; joints stiffen, hair thins to a light floss; numerous cosmetic operations have lifted their face so many times their eyebrows are on the back of their head somewhere, leaving the skin pulled so tight about their cheeks that their lips are fixed into a permanent clown's grin.

What is worse, they are not left to grow old and to face oblivion in peace. The press can smell decay a mile off, and critics, knowing when a veteran actress's career is on the skids, are not slow to tell her so publicly, dismissing her as a has-been, and so taking her one inevitable notch further along the Rainbow.

All that effort, all those years of forced glamour, razzle-dazzle, anguish and pretence, and where has it got her? A life-achievement award from this or that academy, honorary membership of such-and-such an institute, freedom of some obscure town in Illinois that doesn't even have a McDonald's it's so remote, and a grave at the posh end of the cemetery, alongside her pet chihuahua and the remains of her last three husbands.

It is not a pleasant life at the end of the Success Rainbow.

And this is by no means confined to over-the-hill actresses alone; it applies also to the ageing past-it actor. One year they worship the water he walks on, the next he is forgotten, such is the nature of the profession. Loving appreciation can never be pinned down. It shifts and moves onwards, and so must the actor, otherwise, sure as anything, he will get left behind. Before he knows it, he too has been shunted down another couple of pegs on the Rainbow.

The trouble is that there are too many thespians around these days. A glut of non-entities exists in the acting world: aspiring performers with unlimitless talent, who were pushed on to the stage as toddlers by desperately super-optimistic mothers, hoping to give their little Toby or Amanda a chance they themselves never had, and who already believe quite fiercely that the next Pia Zadora or Christopher Atkins is sitting right there on their lap. Quite often, they *are* too.

Thus propelled by Mom, they take their first step in the business at three months old in nappy commercials, wobbling about and picking their bottoms to music. If they're not too disillusioned by the time they reach infancy, they begin the standard day-in day-out round of engagements – more kiddie commercials, attending stage school as they grow older, trying for auditions, making even more commercials, filling in time until they can do their required stint in repertory, get their Equity Card and get out to start earning some money. Many of them find a job right away in the West End, usually serving hamburgers in fast-food restaurants by day and selling programmes to theatre audiences by night, waiting for their big break.

To many unemployed actors with flair and talent, this makes the situation even more frustrating. The competition is so oppressive, yet they are serious about their ability, and eager to get on; ever since they were a foetus, all they *ever* wanted to do was act; to be lifted above the heads of the hoi-poloi, all of whom, unfortunately, share the same desire – to be cheered and applauded, fêted by the press and recognized in Safeway. But it is not merely enough to have a flair for acting. An actor with flair is like a pig with a kite – useless. There are hundreds of out-of-work actors with flair, running around Manhattan restaurants serving tacos to out-of-work directors with flair. To make it to the top takes more than ability.

You've got to have presence, conviction, experience, individuality, determination, motivation and nice teeth. And that's the minimum. Or, alternatively, you have to have a trick that somehow makes you stand out from the riff-raff, which is why, if you *are* an actor who classes himself as a 'nobody' on the Success Rainbow but who wants to go places, schmovie-going is a Godsend. Club members have collected vital information from 50 years of movie-making that will help you get noticed and thereby boost your chances of stardom, saving you having to sleep around unnecessarily.

Remember, acting talent can be divided into three broad categories – competent, good and great.

A competent actor *pretends* he is someone else.
A good actor *believes* he is someone else.
A great actor *is* someone else!

Schmovie-going can't make a competent actor into a good one, but it can help the unknown performer with big ideas climb a stage further on the Success Rainbow. For the purposes of what follows, I am assuming that you have the basic wherewithal to be taken on as a humble extra in a film. Make it that far, and let the rules of schmovie-going do the rest.

Extras

The extras are the crowd, the passers-by, pedestrians paid to do as they're told on a set or location, to look busy, remain in the background and ignore the camera.

When you see the dozens of anxious relatives in a film, pacing a fog-bound aerodrome, awaiting news of a plane crash, or tourists criss-crossing a hotel foyer, or the insignificant heads bobbing behind Mark Antony's chariot as it pulls into Rome, those are the extras: human livestock herded into town squares to cheer a hanging, or driven on to the prairies in wagons to be ritually slaughtered by the Cherokees (most of whom are also extras, incidentally). That chorus of chanting peasants winding down the Norwegian hillside in turnip carts, miming to the music on the soundtrack, panicking villagers in disaster movies, circus audiences. . .they are all hired specially to sing or flee or applaud or whatever it is they're doing.

Basically, they can be divided into two sorts, frolickers and non-frolickers.

Frolickers

These are the people in big-budget musicals who appear from nowhere, waving their caps, and cheering when a coach comes in, or a ferry-boat docks, or a parade passes by. Frolickers are jolly, forgiving, trouble-free citizens, always smiling and overjoyed, who will run out to greet anything you send their way – stagecoaches, paddle-steamers, trains, whatever; a body of ready revellers forever on standby just in case anything exciting should happen. They will line the route of a high-speed car-chase, run together in groups to point at strange fireballs in the sky, muttering to each other, 'A UFO. I'm sure it is. Wouldn't you say? A UFO, a UFO.'

> *The Corn is Green* (1945) The only person in the Welsh village of Glansarno who can read is the post mistress. Everyone else is completely illiterate , which hardly explains why the walls of the village are covered with posters, and whenever another one is pasted up people turn out from all corners to read what it says.

In a frolicking situation, listen carefully, and you will always hear a key-phrase that triggers off the rush, such as, 'Wow! A flying saucer!' or, 'Hey, there's a coach comin' in!'

'A coach? Arrivin' *here?*'

And that's all it takes. Out they come, clicking their heels, bouncing little children on their shoulders and singing in unison – a blizzard of happy faces, acting for all they are worth, which isn't much.

Non-Frolickers

By contrast, you have the more serious arm of the extras brigade, brought in usually to flee from erupting volcanoes with their belongings tied to a home-made stretcher, or to scurry for shelter during a bombing raid, or dive behind high walls out of the path of an oncoming tidal wave. They are not given any lines to speak; all they have to do is scream a lot, look frenzied and run about in a constant state of panic. They will also be called upon to fill backlot streets, by strolling up and down and looking into shop windows.

> *Thoroughly Modern Millie* (1967) During the title sequence as Julie Andrews swans down the streets of New York, rearranging her image, the man who is ushering the extras along, making sure they bustle past the camera in sufficient numbers, is reflected in 'The Silhouette Shop' window.

There does come a time when the non-frolicking has to stop, however. It's not all fun for these people.

Because they are so insignificant, it means that they are the first to get it between the eyes in a war film if the plot takes a downturn, and the first to come to grief when the arrows start to fly in an Indian uprising. Non-frolickers in these instances, are called in to form a force of volunteer dead, whose bodies can be strewn across battlefields, left to litter the trenches, and who are always on hand for post-holocaust disarray, genocide and massacres, or any hard-fought battles where both sides sustain large-scale losses. They are troops brought in not to fight, but specifically to fall and lie motionless face down in the dirt until the cameras are switched off. Each one a confirmed stretcher-case before a single bullet has been fired. They are known collectively as 'the readily-deadlies' (though sometimes called other things: The Queen's Own Casualty Regiment, the Blacks and Blues etc.).

As an acting force, they're highly organized, very much along the lines of a real army, since it is a highly specialized job and recognized as such. We try not to allow politics to creep into schmovie-going, but most enschmoviasts believe that the point the readily-deadlies make is a reasonable one, that if we spent as much time averting wars as we do in honouring the dead after them, then the world might be a safer place. On the plus side, they hold old boys' reunions, run a network of very famous nursing homes for ex-casualties, and have a motto, which has changed many times over the years. It began as 'Who threw that?', was later changed to 'No wars, no fear' when a serious pacifist element gained control, dampening their militarist fervour, then 'Lives before pride' and finally settled for what it is now – 'Who dares, dies!'

Any ambitious actor joining the non-frolickers is faced with a disturbing dilemma. If he performs his job well, and does exactly as the director asks, he will almost surely sink into the background, disappearing among the masses and may never be recognized by the people who matter. On the other hand, if he performs badly he *will* be noticed, but by the wrong people, the film-crew, and possibly be dumped as a foolish amateur. So, with only a brief moment in which to shine and to claim his share of posterity, he needs a quick and cunning way to be noticed. Ten seconds is all he may have, time only for one exaggerated gesture, a prolonged swing of the arm, that extra nod of the head that says, 'Yoo-hoo! Here I am – over here!'

Subtlety is all in this game, so no waving at the camera is allowed, no shifting props to let the audience get a better look at you, and no sly glances into the lens, mouthing 'Hello Mum'. These are the basics. After that, it is up to you what you do. You might like to adopt one of the methods listed below. Schmovie buffs have drawn up an impressive Nine-Point Plan for getting noticed in films, based on how other actors, either by accident or as a result of their own connivance, drew attention to themselves.

1. If you find yourself in amongst a group of milling peasants, for example, it makes sense to mill a little more than everyone else. Chat excitedly, roll your eyes, nudge your neighbour and point at something out of shot. If you think you have slipped into an unfavourable corner, then dodge out of view around the back of the set and enter from the other side. If you are just one figure in a large

madding crowd, be sure to mad more aggressively than those around you. Make a nuisance of youself. They can't cut the whole scene out, and even if they remove a part of it, you're bound to be in a high proportion of what's left.

> *The Bandwagon* (1953) When Fred Astaire performs his 'Shine on Your Shoes' number in a run-down New York amusement arcade, the frolicking extras in the background have got the right idea about being noticed. In the end, you find yourself watching *them* rather than Astaire, and counting the number of times they succeed in working themselves into shot.
>
> A little boy in a plaid shirt, with sticky-up hair, makes eight separate appearances, a pair of sailors manage ten between them, a young girl in a maroon cardigan turns up eight times, and an obese middle-aged tart clutching a black handbag squeezes herself into view a whole nine times, running across the back, playing with the props, jostling her way past the camera, laughing and fooling around, very much the star of the piece for us.

2. Another good way is to throw yourself to the floor as soon as the camera is on you, preferably when everyone else is standing to attention.

> *Alexander the Great* (1956) One soldier positioned in the front line of the Persian Army steps back as Richard Burton approaches, overbalances and falls down.

No rules for this – it's a matter of timing and luck, but best used in a scene too vast and too costly to reshoot, in which case if your little performance is the only blot on the shot, they may let it through. If, by chance, the story takes place in a theatre, wait until the actors on stage receive a standing ovation, then sit down quickly and talk to a friend *(The Bandwagon* again).

3. If you are supposed to be dead or unconscious, either move some part of your body to show the audience that you're only acting after all or, even better, get up and walk about.

> *Son of Ali Baba* (1952) A dead man, lying flat on the ground while the fight continues around him, stays completely still until he thinks that someone is about to

tread on his arm, then moves it quickly out of the way. (See also The Utility Stiff.)

4. Give a facial reaction to events going on around you that is totally at odds with the prevailing mood. If everyone else is cheerful and festive, then snarl, or adopt a deadpan expression. Conversely, if the rest are all gloomy and downcast, sport a broad grin or stand sniggering at the back *(Vera Cruz)*.

   Alexander the Great (1956) During a battle between the Persians and the Greeks, two men fighting each other are smiling and laughing and having a jolly old time at the back. Elsewhere another man takes his sword and needles an opponent playfully in the arm with it just for fun.

   Arm of Fire (1964) Another battle, this time in 800BC. Three men sitting on horses towards the back of the troops are waving their swords slowly and indifferently while they smile lazily and chatter amongst themselves.

5. Die twice if possible. Always a bright idea, giving you two bites at the recognition cherry, although the success of your plan lies very much in the hands of the editor. He could easily realize what you are up to and cut you out!

   Attila the Hun (1954) One of the Roman soldiers, standing apart from the rest of the men, dies twice, on both occasions with an arrow in the chest.

6. Be the only character in an historical film to wear a wristwatch.

   El Cid (1961) At the siege of Valencia in twelfth-century Spain, bread is catapulted over the city walls to feed the starving inhabitants, and as a crowd of non-frolicking extras reaches out for the loaves one of them is wearing a watch with an elasticated metal band.

Alternatively, and in the right circumstances, leaving your watch off can achieve a similar effect.

Land of the Pharaohs (1955) One of the Pharaoh's sun-tanned fan-bearers has a clear white band around his wrist where he usually wears a watch when he's not filming historical epics.

7. Act out of phase with everyone else, I:

North by Northwest (1959) In the cafeteria at the Mount Rushmore monument, as the film is reaching its climax, Cary Grant is shot in the shoulder by Eva Marie Saint. But before she takes out the gun, and before anyone around her even knows she is carrying one, a little boy seated at a table sticks his fingers in his ears, waiting for the bang. He obviously recalls how loud it was at rehearsals.

8. Act out of phase with everyone else, II:

Attila the Hun (1954) To entertain a visiting Roman envoy, Attila organizes a midnight feast and a friendly sparring match around the campfire. As a schmoviebuff, I can tell you that your interest lies not in the men wrestling with each other in the foreground, but in the man wrestling alone with a piece of meat on a spit in the background. Either the spit snapped before filming began, or it never worked at all, because when he turns the handle the carcass does not move, except for very occasionally. The rest of the time, no matter how vigorously he turns the handle, the carcass hangs motionless over the flames.

Ulysses (1954) A highly suspicious coincidence this. Made by the same company, and in the same year, and featuring the same mis-take. The spit this time is in Ulysses' camp. One of his men is turning the handle quite diligently, but to no avail. The carcass won't budge an inch.

9. Be a passer-by who passes by more than anyone else does.

The Young Ones (1961) Cliff Richard and his pals are sitting in a high-street cafe working on a script for their new show. The scene outside the window is miserable: pouring rain and a few pedestrians hurrying past with umbrellas. But with only a limited number of non-frolickers to rush past the window, the same people are obliged to make the journey several times. To this end, two routes have been devised. The first is the simplest and involves simply walking back and forth close to the set. The second route takes them around the back of a line of railings a few yards away, where they sneak past with heads down and collars up ready to come past the window a second time. To make them look a little different each turn, some of them swap brollies before they return. All very clever, and once you know what they're up to, the most entertaining part of the entire film.

As an actor, what you do after this depends largely on whether you succeeded in getting yourself noticed or not. If you did, well done! You may now pass quickly on to the second rung of the ladder, which is covered in the next chapter. If you didn't, then you should either try again by adopting a fresh ruse from those set out above and see how far you get next time; or, bitterly enraged at being ignored, you could give up, and apply to join a secret guerrilla organization calling itself the Society of Film Saboteurs (SFS), a crack unit of interfering busy-bodies and intruders, who make it their life's work to appear in as many movies as they possibly can without the director or anyone else realizing they are there.

No one knows precisely what their house rules are – they are so closely guarded – but at least three of them are quite obvious. To be considered successful as a film saboteur, you must a) be featured clearly in the finished print of a major motion picture; b) whenever possible, be looking directly into the camera, and c) try to be wearing something white. White is not essential, but it is their trademark, which is why we suspect that the little guy in the white overalls in *The World, the Flesh and the Devil* (1959) is an undercover SFS operative. We can't be sure because the identity of all members, as well as where they meet and how they make contact, are still complete mysteries. What we do know is that they are a smallish group of vexatious and resentful actors who never made it to the big-time, and who are reeking revenge in the only way they know how – by ruining scenes in other people's films.

This makes our job in spotting them impossibly difficult. If you don't know who they are, how the hell do you spot them or, for that matter, how do you tell them apart from ordinary members of the public? All I can do is give you a few examples of their work, scenes with intruders in them, and leave you to fathom out for yourself who is an SFS member and who isn't.

From what we know of their activities, they seem to have three main lines of attack.

Reflection

Quite apart from deliberate provocation on the SFS's part, mirrors of any sort or size have always caused problems in films.

> *Funny Girl* (1968) A black-tie audience is watching a song-and-dance number in a theatre. On the stage is a young girl in a bathtub full of suds. Behind her a column of elegant long mirrors recedes slowly to allow the rest of the dancers through. As the mirrors move back, they should, if all is well, give a clear reflection of the audience in the stalls. But luckily, all is not well. Not only do they reveal that there is no audience, but also that there isn't a theatre either. Just a cable and some backstage equipment.

> *Land of the Pharaohs* (1955) Jack Hawkins returns to his palace in Egypt with sand clogging every pore. He takes a bath, then gazes into a mirror held by one of his hand-maidens, who tilts it at such an angle that you can see over the top of the set.

It need not be mirrors that cause trouble. Some surfaces are so highly reflective that they let you see everything going on all around them, including behind the camera.

Star! (1968) Sir Anthony Spencer, a potential husband for Gertrude Lawrence, stands in her bedroom wearing the gleaming breast-plate of his Coldstream Guards uniform, which is so highly polished that with every turn it reveals new wonders – where the camera is, where the set ends, the lights, the crew, everything.

Logan's Run (1976) Michael York and Jenny Agutter are confronted in some ice-caverns by a chrome-plated robot, bright silver and shiny to the point of being a menace. Whichever way it faces, it reflects an arc lamp here, a gantry there, and oh look! – there are three members of the film crew huddled in a tight group around the camera!

The same applies to anything silver, such as a lampshade (*Airport '75*, 1974); a soup tureen (*A New Leaf*, 1970); or things made of glass, a pair of sunglasses perhaps (*Nightwing*, 1979; *For Your Eyes Only*, 1981; *Absence of Malice*, 1983; and *I, the Jury*, 1982); a shop-window (*Carmen Jones*, 1954); or any other kind of window come to that (*Fuzz*, 1972; *All That Heaven Allows*, 1955; *The Cannonball Run*, 1981; and *When Time Ran Out*, 1980).

The hardest knock of all comes when great care is taken to avoid a stray reflection that they know might spoil a scene, and they are then beaten by circumstance.

The Man With the Golden Gun (1974) A fight breaks out backstage in a Beirut nightclub. James Bond (Roger Moore) is set upon by three henchmen in a darkened dressing-room. During the scrap, one of the henchies flies sideways and hits the dressing-table, knocking it askew to reflect the entire camera crew and showing us that the fourth wall of the room is missing. Naturally, they are not slow to rectify the error, and the dressing-table is back in place by the next shot.

Members of the SFS play on this basic weakness to the fullest extent. By wearing white, their reflection shows up more clearly, making them easier to spot when it comes to proving that an assignment has been successfully completed.

Where the Bullets Fly (1966) As a porter pastes an 'All seats reserved' sticker to the window of a train on

Waterloo Station, a man in a short-sleeved white shirt is reflected in the window beside him. He's quite plump, over 50 and very obvious.

Kiss of the Vampire (1962) In this one it was a woman in a white frock reflected in the glass of a carriage.

Expresso Bongo (1959) When a Rolls-Royce pulls into the forecourt of the Dorchester Hotel in London, a man in a flat cap is reflected in the grille. He is crouching audaciously under the camera and even seems to have got hold of a microphone!

I don't feel I need to give you a list of SFS activities. Once you start watching out for their intrusions, you will clock up many examples of your own. You might like to take a look at *Vice Squad* (1953), where one operative appears, smoking, in the quarter-light of a parked car, and *The Hunter* (1980), where he appears, fiddling with the camera, reflected in a pane of glass in Eli Wallach's office. Other unconfirmed sightings may be found in *Halloween* (1978), *Forbidden Planet* (1956), *Thoroughly Modern Millie* (1967), *The Rose* (1979), and *The Four Seasons* (1981).

Reaction

Next step up from reflection has got to be the full-blown cameo appearance. This is considered more of an achievement by the SFS, but it's a toughie. There are not many opportunities for an agent to step directly into shot and stare into the lens, but it happens now and again.

Assault on Precinct 13 (1976) A police officer on his way by car to his new assignment takes instructions as he cruises along the highway. A black woman driver in sunglasses, who is either an SFS agent or else a member of the public with extraordinary presence of mind, pulls up alongside his car and looks straight into the camera. He draws ahead and loses her. Next minute, she pulls into view a second time and looks in, only to fall behind again. But, undaunted, back she comes, and peers into the car for a third time.

It Started in Naples (1960) The man in the white shirt is standing leaning against a wall outside Naples station, with his hands behind his back.

The King of Comedy (1983) Perhaps the longest stint by an alleged member of the SFS in front of the camera. It happens when Robert De Niro stands on a New York street arguing with his rather sick girlfriend. An old guy in a white shirt makes full use of the situation, positioning himself in shot and standing there, looking directly into the camera for probably 10 to 15 seconds. Their greatest success to-date.

Attack of the Crab Monsters (1957) Following a nuclear test, crabs on an uncharted Pacific atoll grow to enormous proportions. Now, I don't think I shall be spoiling the effect of this film for anyone if I tell you that the giant crabs are really just big puppets operated from underneath by a few stage-hands, who walk around with them on their shoulders. One of them is wearing a pair of white trousers. You can see his legs as the crab scuttles away along the beach at the end of the picture.

Repetition

The most difficult trick of the lot is for an SFS member to appear in a scene, fall over twice and manage to be left in the film after doing so. Those who manage it must surely receive the maximum points from the Society on whatever scoring system they use.

Sea Wife (1957) The passengers on a sinking ship make a mad dash to the lifeboats. One boat becomes so overcrowded that it snaps from the winch and spills all the people in it into the water. One man in a white boiler suit falls out of the boat twice in consecutive shots.

Tora! Tora! Tora! (1970) During a raid on an airfield, a large explosion rips up the runway, and a small maintenance engineer in white overalls has to scramble away to safety. This is followed by another explosion, from a different angle, and the same guy scrambles away again.

The Blob (1958) A man in a pink suit and white hat trips over as he runs out of a cinema, then almost at once runs out again and trips over in exactly the same place.

A Show of Hands

A Show of Hands

It's a fun, fun life in the chor-us;
Fun is what the chorus life's about,
With no perks, no lines, no credit,
You can bet the man who said it,
Was doin' the best he could – to get out!

(*Whose Shoes Are Those?*, 1948)

No committed actor with an eye on the big-time is going to want to remain in the chorus for long. He knows he must move on, and if he manages to bring himself to the attention of the director and shows promise, he may well be plucked out of the crowd and handed a small part to play – nothing much to begin with, functional rather than prestigious, but enough to carry his name into the bottom end of the closing credits for the first time. He may even be given a line of dialogue to speak.

The people who play the bit-parts, these insignificant in-between roles, may be mere plankton on the surface of the acting pond, but without them, a director would have no one to drive the leading lady's carriage up to the squire's house; no innkeeper to tether her mare; no butler to pull open the library doors and say, 'Professor Faltskog to see you, Sir', or 'Will Madam be taking tea on the terrace this afternoon, or on the lawn?'; no newspaper-vendor to stand on a street corner and shout out, purely for the audience's benefit, that a madman is on the loose; nobody to cry, 'There's a coach comin' in!' and set the frolickers off.

You could probably list 100 of them all-told, but for the purposes of schmovie-going and this book, you need only concentrate on six, and those are the ones listed in the Cliché Code.

1. The Despairing Hag

This is the bedraggled woman in Westerns who runs from a dusty doorway in shawl and sandles to snatch her child out of the path of oncoming troops or rampaging wild cattle. She is usually billed as the '4th peasant' and has clocked up numerous appearances over the years in films from *This Land Is Mine* (1943) to *Vera Cruz* (1953). You may also find her picking through the rubble after an air raid in war films, or panicking on a busy street as her pram runs towards fast-moving traffic *(The Bishop's Wife*, 1947), or about to be crushed by a falling girder *(Superman II*, 1980), but wherever she is, she is always bleating the same old line, 'My baby! My baby!'

In some cases, she is no more than a scapegoat for a worried director, stumped for what to do next, who needs a little extra touch to add zest to a dreary scene. But he can't fool us: enschmoviasts know what he's up to, which is why you will sometimes hear a ripple of applause from the front stalls when a tiny child is about to be trampled by tearaway horses, and cries of 'Shame!' when his mother, the despairing hag, runs out to rescue him.

2. Reactioneers

If a reactioneer turns up in a comedy film, this tells you that a measure of panic has set in behind the camera. Things are not going well.

These people are brought in to a scene to look suitably confounded or annoyed when something outrageous happens around them, in the street, in a hotel lobby or in their back garden. A variety of reactions is on offer here: they may drop their jaw, scratch their head, give a quizzical twist of the lip, let go of whatever they are carrying, walk absentmindedly into a pillar or fall down a manhole. Basically, it is the director's last chance to squeeze a chuckle out of a situation that he fears may not be quite as funny on the screen as it looked in the script.

All kinds of characters have been used for this in the past, from window-cleaners to policemen on point-duty ('Well, I'll be. . .'), but in practice, film-makers generally opt for one of three:

a) The bald, middle-aged bachelor with the pop-eyes, who 'happens' to be wandering down a corridor in his dressing-gown, carrying a mug of hot milk, when seven giggling Filipino women covered all over in stamp-hinges and putty run out of Leo's room chased by a gorilla on stilts. The reactioneer's job is to rescue a dire, unwitty shot like this. He will stop in his tracks, ogle for a second with his pop-eyes, drop the mug, and then give 'The Look' direct to camera – an expression of the sort one normally associates with brain-death.

warrrrrrp-warrrrp-warrrrp-warrrp-waaaarrp!

b) He has a female counterpart, the frustrated snoopy shrew, in the hair-net and nightdress, who patrols the same sort of territory waiting to be shocked, and shows an appreciable degree of alarm at excessive kissing between man and wife in public, or 'happens' to peek through her curtains at home when two naked French sailors leapfrog through her vegetable patch. A different character, but same procedure: she will stop, ogle, drop what she is carrying, then give 'The Look'.

waaarrrrrp-waarrarrrrrp-waaarrrrp-waaaarrp!

c) The good-time alcoholic (whose name eight times out of ten will be Harvey!) on his twentieth Pernod of the evening, who looks out of the window and sees three geese drop past it on parachutes. He is the stock drunk, dressed in shabby overcoat, pork pie hat cocked at an unhealthy angle, shirt collar sticking out awkwardly from under his jacket, and lots of stubble. When the situation calls for more than outrage, and something along the lines of disbelief verging on wide-eyed stupor, this is your man. He will hold up his cider-bottle, stare at it, give 'The Look' to the camera, and then throw the bottle back over his shoulder, shaking his head.

warrrrrrp-waaaarrrrrrp-warrrpp-waaaarrrrp!

All three tend to be underscored by this crowing trumpet accompaniment, a piece of crude punctuation, and the director's way of saying to the audience, 'Laugh, dammit! This is *funny*!', when he knows full well it isn't.

3. Gonners

'Gonner' is the name given to any character in a film who has obviously been earmarked for an early death.

It is well known that when a psychopathic axeman is on the loose around a neighbourhood, he always begins by butchering those actors who appear at the bottom of the cast-list, knocking them off one at a time and working his way gradually up the credits, as a taster of what lies in store for the principal actors if he isn't caught quickly.

Murder mysteries, especially, need outbreaks of random violence at regular intervals to keep the story ticking over, and to remind the audience that the killer is still at large/means business/is fiendish and invincible/will stop at nothing. The average knock-off rate for victims in thrillers is consequently about one every twenty minutes, and the people who play them are called gonners. Gonners are the surely-deads, the same people who selfishly overcrowd lifeboats until they tip into the sea, or pack out elevators in burning buildings until they are so full, the cable breaks and they all plunge down the shaft. When they are hired, somewhere in the contract they sign, gobbled up in the mass of small print, is supposedly a provision called the Gonner Clause, indicating that the character they are to play will be slaughtered within minutes of his first appearance on screen.

The speed of their demise is governed by two factors: how much they are being paid, and how far down the credits they are.

You should have no problem spotting gonners in mystery films, or in any other kind of film for that matter. But to help start you off, here is the complete gonner-spotter's checklist. Armed with the information set out below, you should be able to astound whole cinemas full of people as you predict with uncanny precision who in the cast will die first.

a) Peasants. Film-makers take the greatest delight in killing peasants, and never miss an opportunity to shoot them, mine them, bomb them, strafe them or set them alight. Which is why, in war films, whenever a line of helpless peasants is filing across a field or down a country road, enemy fighter planes will almost certainly swoop out of the skies and shoot the lot of them dead. These are the actors who had a gonner clause in their contract, and it helps if at least a third of them are crippled women in broken moccasins, with babies strapped to their back, or dirty starving orphans, as they usually make for an extra heart-string-tugger, though this is by no means essential.

Strafing is reserved mostly for down-and-outs – the poor people, refugees and such, though on occasions, it has been known to happen to a line of soldiers. (In *The Longest Day* (1962), it was two columns of German infantrymen marching along the roadside who were shot at.) But characters are never strafed unless they are walking in single file. If the crowd are milling haphazardly, then they must be set upon by Nazi stormtroopers with rifles, or gunned down from a passing lorry. In *Night of the Generals* (1967) the citizens running willy-nilly across a large square have to be rounded up by the Germans and decimated as a job-lot.

The aerial attack has three distinct advantages in this context: first, it fulfils a basic need that a director has to kill peasants, and can be counted on to wipe out dozens of them at a time, leaving the rest in such a state that they are unlikely to make it to the end of the story alive. Second, as a plot device, it underlines the menace of the enemy, proving that the Luftwaffe are pretty mean cookies to be sure, and have no time for dirty starving orphans or crippled women in moccasins. Third, it kills off all the gonners outright which, from a financial point of view, is a very sound tactic indeed. The director can rid the plot of all the cheap peripheral characters once they have outlived their usefulness, leaving the better-paid ones to struggle on unharmed.

b) Parachutists. Again in war films, when a top secret and highly dangerous mission calls for a night-time parachute jump behind enemy lines the team sent out to achieve it will be a crack unit made up of five international stars – big names, preferably of mixed British and American origin to widen its appeal at the box-office – plus a couple of gonners, nondescript actors you have never seen before, who will be treated as key members of the unit until shortly after the mission starts when one of them will break his neck on landing or get stuck up a tree and die of exposure, while the other will persevere for another few minutes, only to be brutally tortured by the enemy to show how ruthless they are. In short, anyone sent out on one of these 'You know you might not come back alive. . .' missions, whose face you don't recognize, will not come back alive. The bigger the pay cheque, the longer they last, it's as simple as that.

c) The Homesick Family Man. Directors won't waste any time telling you about a character's background and lifestyle unless it is truly relevant to the story. So when a soldier fighting on the front line takes out a crumpled photograph of his wife and children and shows it to his comrades, that man is a gonner, you can bet on it. What is more, they will waste no time in killing him after this – quickly, before you forget what he's told you and you lose sympathy for him.

d) The Holiday Hopeful. Closely allied to the above, any demoralized soldier in a war film who announces that he is down for a spot of leave in the near future and is going to see his family is a guaranteed fatality. Indeed, you can usually say goodbye to him the moment he mentions it. (He is not too far-removed from Lou – remember Lou? He's the fat federal investigator in American homicide pictures, who dies on his last case, usually just days before retirement. A gonner for sure.)

e) The Self-Sac Do-Gooder. A must for any science-fiction fantasy, he is the man who flies in the face of every piece of evidence there is and insists that plainly hostile alien beings are really begging for peace and friendship. Even though they may have wiped out Tokyo and part of the

Netherlands that same afternoon, he shows spontaneous warmth towards them by offering himself as their next target.

A notable example can be found in *The War of the Worlds* (1952) which gave us the self-sacrificing priest, Uncle Matthew. He decides to offer himself to the aliens to prove what a jolly civilized lot we are here on Earth. Stepping into the crater where the Martian craft has buried itself, he starts muttering, 'Though I walk through the valley of the shadow of death. . . I will fear no evil. . .' Of course the Martians are in fits at this. They want blood, they are looking for whole continents to destroy and here's a little guy with a white neck trying to make friends with them. So without any more ado they turn their death-ray on him and blast him to a cinder. And a good thing too.

As an alternative, you may run across the self-sac scientist – the one who has created a really, *really* dangerous warhead, capable of devastation on a multi-continental scale, or a vaccine so potent it could wipe out the population of Red China 10 times over, but insists he wants it used only for the betterment of mankind! He is utterly unable to see the folly of his work until one day somebody points it out to him. Suddenly he is beside himself with panic, and has to be killed off in mysterious circumstances to stop him raising the alarm.

f) The Superstitious Serviceman. Keep a close lookout for anyone in the armed forces who boasts that he carries a talisman for luck whenever he goes out on a life-or-death mission, because, sure as hell, he'll leave it on the mantelpiece at home when he sets off on his very next assignment. He will perish almost at once. The talisman could be anything, a rabbit's foot, a St Christopher, a Maian Lip, even a buttered bagel, it hardly matters. The fact remains that this guy is a gonner and the rest of the cast may as well start planning his funeral while he is still packing his hold-all.

Do remember, though, not to cheer when news of his death arrives. There may be some people sitting around you in the cinema who haven't read this book yet, and won't know why you're so excited. Subdued jollity is a must on these occasions. Try practising it with *The Way to the Stars* (1945), in which Flight Lieutenant David Archdale leaves his lucky lighter on the fireplace back at the mess, and on his next flight is shot down over France.

g) The Self-Sac Senile Old Git. In a moment of great pressure, when lives are at risk and someone is needed to hold the Gestapo at bay while the rest of the cast make their escape, the grey-haired grandad will pipe up with, 'Save yourselves, all of you. I am old. You have your whole life ahead of you. Go on.' Of course, everyone rallies round to persuade him to change his mind, saying things like, 'We're not leaving here without you.' Empty bravado, every word of it, because in the end, they realize they are on to a good thing, that the man's a lunatic, and they will quite happily make off without him. A moment later, the soldiers will break down the door and pump him full of bullets without a second thought, before setting off after the others. Quite conveniently, he won't be mentioned again after that. His sole purpose for being there was to die at that point. Once he has served his purpose, he can be written off.

h) Champions. Anyone in a disaster movie who volunteers to perform an uncalled-for act of heroism, such as running through a burning apartment to fetch help for everyone else, and who justifies his courage by saying he was a world-class pentathlete and should make the run easily, will die while he is doing it.

i) The One-Man Escape Committee. Any prisoner-of-war who makes a sudden impetuous run for freedom will be shot dead immediately.

If these people would only run behind some bushes or a wall and take cover, then one or two of them might survive once in a while. But they never do. They prefer to run out into the open, clearly visible to any patrolling guards – in the somewhat ill-founded belief that the Germans might admire their initiative and let them through just this one time. But the guards aren't fools; they've read the script, they know that these chaps are gonners, and have no hesitation in killing them straight away.

j) Know-all Cowboys. 'We'll camp here tonight. Don't worry about the Indians – they're friendly.' Take the name of any man who says this in a Western, and mark my words, you'll find he has his head on a stick by the morning.

(A point of interest: in the United States, the 10 people above are not referred to as gonners, but as 'crispy critturs', which apparently is army slang for anyone who is seriously burned in wartime.)

4. The BLAAAAAAA!-Man

This is the chap most film-makers choose to start a crisis. He can take on a number of guises: the nervous lookout on a bank-raid who sees the police car pull around the corner of the street: 'Lummy! It's the filth!'; the young sailor bursting on to the bridge: 'Cap'n, the giraffe's got away!'; the pirate in the crow's nest who, after weeks adrift on a calm sea, yells, 'Land off port bow!' He is used predominantly when the plot has slowed down to a stop to make way for some love interest or background information about the characters. It heralds the start of the next exciting bit.

In each case, the orchestra takes its cue from that special line of dialogue: 'Iceberg dead ahead, Sir!' and goes into spasm, letting out a blast of noise on the soundtrack – BLAAAAAAA! It was always a great favourite, too, in the adventure film area – the trunk thrown open on a jungle expedition: 'Harrison, the parchment! It's gone!' BLAAAAAAA!

Or the doc-meet addressed by a sham scientist: 'Gentlemen, there is a crack in the world!' BLAAAAAAA!

But note, the name 'BLAAAAAAA!-Man' is just another tag of convenience. It can quite easily be a woman. For example the blustering matron who bursts into the hospital ward, 'Doctor Brewster! Come quickly! Emergency in surgery!' BLAAAAAAA!

5. The On-Board Navvy

Up until the mid-sixties, all scientific expeditions to lost worlds, forgotten valleys, distant undiscovered tribal villages, uncharted isles or, at a pinch, into outer space, always took with them a man whose specific job it was to state the obvious, a highly trained officer brought along to disinfect the story of anything complicated or technical that the audience might not understand. If, for instance, there was a chance they could be foxed by a strange gadget on board a diving bell, he would step in, take hold of it and say something facile, such as, 'So *this* is the gizmo that will take us to Atlantis, hnn?' – a rather painful plot device intended to make the audience feel at ease in unfamiliar surrounds.

> *Destination Moon* (1950) When the astronauts go into orbit for the first time, the man they have taken along with them to state the obvious peers out of the rocket window down at Earth and exclaims, 'Wow! The geography books are right!'

> *Fire Maidens From Outer Space* (1956) One of the crew on board a spacecraft bound for Jupiter marvels at how small the Earth seems from a distance. 'It's like looking through the wrong end of a telescope!'

> *The Thing From Another World* (1951) An alien creature is running wild in a research station at the North Pole. On analysing its biological make-up, one scientist discovers that it's got an advanced brain but the body of a vegetable, at which point the on-board navvy chips in with, 'An intellectual carrot. The mind boggles!'

> *Red Planet Mars* (1952) A military navvy in a space observatory is amazed by the complexity of the task in contacting the Martians: 'It's like trying to work out a system of communication with a golliwog!'

He may be called on at times to tell us something that is already staring us in the face.

> *War of the Worlds* (1952) As the Martians begin to emerge from their crater, Uncle Matthew, the incendiary holyman and gonner, looks on in wonder and gasps, 'Beings from another world!'

A director may even use him as part of the scene-setting chore, to identify some landmark in a city for the benefit of foreigners who may not have been there.

> *Where the Bullets Fly* (1966) A man climbs into a London taxi and says to the driver, 'Waterloo!' to which the driver replies, 'What? The station?'

Occasionally, the on-board navvy character and the BLAAAAAAA!-Man in a film will be one and the same.

> *Tarantula* (1955) Leo G. Carroll has fallen foul of a serum that causes his body to decompose. The on-board navvy turns up at his laboratory and cries, 'But professor, your face. . .it's. . .' BLAAAAAAA! And sure enough, when he turns round to look at the camera, *it is!*

If you are unsure which member of the cast is the on-board navvy, then look out for a number of tell-tale phrases in the dialogue that give it away. The first is, 'You're not suggesting. . .?'

> *The Deadly Mantis* (1957) Part of a giant flying insect is picked up and examined by experts. It turns out to be a spur from one of its forelegs. When he is told this, the navvy exclaims, 'You're not suggesting it comes from some creature. . .as yet unknown? . . . something incredibly, unbelievably huge?'

Another one is 'You mean. . .?'

> *The Blob* (1958) A meteorite has landed in some woods, and when a group of teenagers finds it, one of them has to be told what it is and where it's come from. 'You mean this pebble's been hot-rodding it around the Universe?'

> *Raiders of the Lost Ark* (1981) Two Army Intelligence men find out that the Lost Ark of the Covenant is where the Hebrews stored the Ten Commandments. One of them, the navvy, can't believe it: 'You mean *the* Ten Commandments?'

There are other lines you should bear in mind. First, the one reserved for anybody who is told something that is quite impossible: 'But. . .that's impossible!' Second, when a villain is about to get away with his fiendish plan: 'You won't get away with this!' is the usual navvy-line; and third, when a character is told that Professor Baxter murdered the girl, the line immediately after will be, 'What are you trying to say?' It's blatantly obvious what he's trying to say, but for the benefit of the Dimwit Element, for whom nothing is too much trouble, he will go on to explain the details of the murder and all relevant clues and circumstances for a second time. I suppose we should be grateful that they care.

Technical terms of any sort are better left out of a film. They can't simply be dropped into the dialogue in the hope that the audience will already know what they mean. Therefore, if any piece of specialized scientific language is mentioned in passing, it must somehow be defined for us before we go much further. Its meaning must be slipped into the conversation, also in passing within the next couple of scenes, and who better for this job than the on-board navvy?

> *Venom* (1981) Sarah Miles plays the resident expert at London's Institute of Toxicology. Having discovered that a small boy has been handed a poisonous snake for a pet, she rings the police. 'This is Marion Stowe. Doctor Marion Stowe of the Institute of Toxicology. . .' she says to the police sergeant on the other end, who takes down the details slowly. 'Tox-ic. . .ology. That's. . .that's poisons, isn't it?' Correct! Hurrraaaaaaaayyyy!

We learned in Chapter Three that journalists make the perfect stooges when it comes to explaining the story-so-far. Well, let me tell you, they also make terrific on-board navvies.

> *War of the Worlds* (1952) Interviewed by a radio reporter as to what the Martians are going to look like, an expert on the spot says, 'They may have more than one brain. . .' 'You mean *two*. . .?' begs the astonished reporter.

6. Exotic Dancers

Part of the burden that most historical epics must bear is the curse of exotic dancing.

The problem facing producers who set out to make this kind of movie was that each time a new one went into production, it had to at least match, if not better, the spectacle created by its predecessors. So that, by the late Fifties, a well-defined shopping list of ingredients had been established dictating what elements had to be included in any such film if it was to make a significant impact at the box-office. The result being that the latest biblical epic would contain everything the previous one had, plus a little extra something to hoist it above the competition.

When these pictures are shown again today, it is possible to check off each ingredient against the list as it turns up in the story. Battles, large scale – three, yes – tick! Love scenes, two – one held surreptitiously in a private garden accompanied by quiet harp music in the background – yes, tick! Years of torment by a great leader exiled into the wilderness – got it, tick! And so on. There had to be at least one truly mammoth set, one that they could boast they had spent a third of the budget on – a life-sized pyramid, Roman town-square, coliseum, amphitheatre, temple or triumphal arch, something to brag about later to the press; a vast chanting crowd scene; a hero with arms as thick as piano accordions, who rescues a slave from the jaws of oppression and is rewarded by friendship for life; a villainous challenger to the throne; bitter squabbles between royal father and son, leading to one of them being stabbed in the palace courtyard or banished from the kingdom for ever; if any mention is made of the Ides of March, a flurry of dead leaves around the actors' feet; a ponderous old sage who, if he wasn't played by Finlay Currie, had to be at least a Finlay Currie lookalike. Indeed, if he wasn't played by Finlay Currie, it probably wasn't as good a picture as they were making out. Then last, and least, the exotic dancers to add licentious revelry to meal-times and all festive occasions.

Producers considered dancers essential to an epic format, yet nobody would ever have missed them if they hadn't been there. The story invariably had to grind to a dead halt to accommodate them, and the main characters simply had to sit down, keep quiet and watch as a dozen floozies in veils and sequins wiggled, weaved and flapped their arms in rough unison, flitting about the set shaking nets, sticks or fans and pelting onlookers with lotus petals and wet sponges. The intention was that they should conjure up a feeling of period authenticity and add a tang of sultry decadence to the picture as a whole, but I can't see that they ever did.

Once they had begun their routine, there was nothing much anybody could do to stop them.

> *Attila the Hun* (1954) Faced with a pack of exotic dancers in his palace, the only way the Roman Emperor can think of to cut short their drab and lifeless performance is by setting a leopard on them.

Part of these dance sequences always had the girls throwing themselves on the floor. The cheaper a film was, the more often they fell to the ground.

> *She-Demons* (1957) A small group of tribal women are dancing clumsily on a beach to a throbbing bongo accompaniment. At the climax, they throw themselves to the ground. One of them stretches out a little too far, pushing all the sand away with her foot to reveal the studio floor underneath.

Some of them were given even more screen-time as they were shown relaxing after the dance.

> *The Wild Women of Wongo* (1958) A bunch of nymphets go for a swim in the ocean. When they are underwater, there are four of them, but when they come up for air, there are five.

Stock Movie Perishables

After all that, you might suppose that the lowest form of life in any picture was either the stock drunks or the readily-deadlies. Surely, nothing could be more demeaning than walking round in a grubby overcoat staring at a cider bottle for a living, or lying face-down in mud, completely forgotten for eight hours a day. Well, in that case, you hadn't counted on a couple of other characters who appear regularly in feature films, often without your knowing they are there, and who have the lousiest jobs of the lot – dummies and stuntmen.

Experience shows that an actor will only take so many risks with his own life before he steps down and lets someone else – someone more expendable – fill his place. The script may ask for the lead character, in the course of his adventures, to fall 14 storeys into the street, or to be tipped down a quarry head-first, or crushed by a runaway truck, but when it comes to the crunch, and pain is in prospect, actors are remarkably slow to volunteer for these duties. So on the odd occasion that they have to be attacked or injured, they insist that every chance of real hurt is removed from the scene, and that they are adequately protected.

Blood on Satan's Claw (1970) Michele Dotrice is chased through a forest by five men who believe she has been practising the black arts. Between them, they lift her up, then swing her one-two-three, and throw her into a lake. But as they let go, a large right hand drops down into the top half of the picture, blocking the view: either to prevent her hitting the camera and damaging a very expensive piece of equipment, or, less likely, to catch her before she hurts herself on the ground. We may never know which.

Actors who do have to be injured for art's sake, will normally be quite well-protected – against a sword in the heart perhaps. . .

Knights of the Round Table (1953) During a battle between King Arthur's army and Mordred's, one warrior takes his sword and runs it through the chest of Mordred's standard-bearer, but the sword more than obviously just slips straight under the bearer's right armpit, missing his chest completely.

. . .an arrow in the back. . .

Custer of the West (1968) When Custer's men are trapped in a circle by the Indians, one of the soldiers gets shot in the back with an arrow, but it doesn't kill him, because he had the presence of mind to stick a thick cork pad inside his shirt beforehand to catch it.

. . .or in the chest. . .

Run of the Arrow (1956) In this one, the arrow strikes a man full in the chest but, luckily, he too has a pad under his shirt to stop it touching him.

. . .or a bullet in the spine. . .

The Klansman (1974) At a civil rights rally in Alabama, one of the spectators is shot in the back, but the bullet strikes him smack on that large pad he has got stuck beneath his clothes.

When actors are handling weapons, they also take the greatest care in case they hurt someone with them.

Alexander the Great (1956) In the thick of a battle between the Athenians and the Macedonians, General Neville holds his spear much as one might carry a shopping bag. He starts to throw it, then realizes that, if he does, it might just hit somebody, so he plays safe, finds a convenient spot and throws it to the ground.

Dummies

No amount of cajoling, it seems, will persuade an actor to have a limb severed in order to play a role more effectively; which is why, after a character loses his hand in a film, once the stump has been treated and bandaged, both his arms are always the same length again *(Hawk the Slayer,* 1980; *Attack of the Crab Monsters,* 1957).

The Incredible Melting Man (1977) An astronaut suffering from advanced radiation sickness has his arm chopped off with a meat cleaver. But when he runs away, the arm is clearly stuffed up the front of his shirt.

And Now the Screaming Starts (1973) Silas, the happy-go-not-so-lucky woodcutter, has his hand chopped off by Herbert Lom as a punishment. But it looks as though losing the hand immediately makes the top of his arm swell to twice its normal size, where he has doubled it up inside the sleeve.

If the proposed injury goes beyond the mere loss of a limb, if crushing, burning or mutilation is involved – stunts that would mean an almost certain death for whoever tried them – then, quite simply, nobody wastes time trying them. Instead they send for a dummy.

When the going gets tough, the tough get stand-ins!

Dummies have definite merits in any crisis. Most of them will stare hell in the face quite impassively and can be subjected to untold levels of punishment without flinching. Incapable of panic, they will fall off high bridges into rapids *(Royal Flash,* 1975), dive over cliffs in unstoppable cars *(Eat My Dust,* 1976), crash their jeep into a ditch and be thrown through the windscreen *(Where Eagles Dare,* 1969), fly headlong out of exploding power-boats *(Moonraker,* 1979), or be jettisoned off crashed motorbikes *(King of the Rocketmen,* 1949), and not show the slightest hint of alarm.

But on the demerit side, dummies always look like dummies – lifeless flimsy-limbed mannequins; they rarely, if ever, resemble human beings. Either because they are given the wrong bodyweight, and are so heavy they plummet to the ground in half a second, or so light that their body is taken up by pockets of air as they fall, so that they flutter from side to side on the way down; alternatively, because the padding inside is wrongly distributed, which means that they drop wrist-first, turning neck-over-thigh in a crazy swastika-shape before hitting the ground in a heap. Some of them would not look half as bad on film if the camera didn't linger on them for quite so long.

> *MacKenna's Gold* (1969) A dummy Indian squaw drops off her horse over the edge of a cliff, and glides in an arc, caught by the wind, legs outstretched, arms waving madly like socks on a washing-line, down, down into the valley below, with the camera lapping up every laughable contortion as she falls.

> *Light at the Edge of the World* (1971) Kirk Douglas jumps over a cliff and is replaced for the actual drop by a dummy with stiff little legs that drifts gracefully down to the sea, its arms twisting and rotating as though it were conducting a violin concerto.

> *The Last Voyage* (1960) An explosion tears through the engine room of the cruise liner *SS Claridon* and blows out the floor of the dining-room on the deck above. A dummy in a red sweater, sitting on top of the blast, is catapulted through the air. The poor thing has been given no legs, so its trousers flap comically as it sails across the room and lands on its head behind the piano.

Dummies are traditionally given those appalling glued-on hairpieces, the shining synthetic ones usually worn in the street by pensioners with too much pride to show their baldness, but not enough to know when they look ridiculous. (The most favourite brand, I'm reliably informed, is the 'Stick-in-a-tick' Skullhugger Deluxe, but I wouldn't like to recommend it, having seen some of the films it appears in – *Airport '75*, 1974, being one.)

> *The Longest Day* (1962) In 1944, the Germans are obviously expecting the British and American assault on the Normandy beaches because, as this film shows, they have gone to the trouble of filling their gun-positions with dummies and scattering a large number of readily-deadlies across the shore for effect.

Robert Wagner runs up the beach to knock out one of those gun positions. He tosses a hand-grenade into the bunker, which explodes, knocking the real German soldiers tamely to one side, and leaving the dummies in front to bear the brunt of the blast. One of them somersaults right out of shot, arms and legs wagging, while his stuffed buddy cartwheels rigidly over the cliff-edge and bounces on to his head.

Paths of Glory (1957) Set in France again, but during World War I: a dead soldier is sprawled on the ground, well in shot, with hunky square shoulders, flat arms and a backpack chock-full of explosives. The moment the camera is on him, he blows up violently. (Dummies are also very obliging!)

We are so used to dummies being substituted for people in stunts, that we never expect the tables to be turned and for a dummy's place to be taken by a real person.

Damnation Alley (1977) After World War III, Jan-Michael Vincent rides into a nearby town to fetch the closest thing he can find to a woman. The closest thing, it turns out, is a dummy from a shop-window display. He props it up on his motorbike and carries it back to base. But this is bumpy desert terrain, and it looks as though the dummy must have fallen off the bike each time it moved, so for a short sequence during the journey, the dummy is replaced by a real woman. I suppose they thought she would never be spotted from a distance ('It's a long-shot, but it might just work. . .')

To be crushed, burned, blown to bits, or dropped from a very great height, that is the dummy's lot. For anything less dangerous, and indeed more lifelike, they will usually turn to an experienced stuntman for help.

Stuntmen

A stuntman will fall down a staircase for you or throw himself under a passing lorry. In fact, it is his greatest pleasure to get hurt. Treat him rough, box his ears, set him on fire and he'll love you for it. He's like a playful kitten when his life's at stake. Give him enough rope and he'll hang himself. Give him enough attention and he will let you fire a crossbow dart into his arm or set wild unfed dogs on him. If you meet one of these chaps at a party, he will feel quite affronted if you don't ask him to stick his tongue into a live electric light socket at least once during the evening.

A dummy can't leap off a verandah and on to the one next door; he can't run along the roof of a train, hopping from carriage to carriage; he can't jump from one horse to another when a posse is heading the outlaws off at the pass – a dummy is incapable of many feats that only a dummy would try and do. So for the foolishly reckless jobs on a film, they bring in a stuntman. In that way, their action sequences look more vivid, and more realistic.

These guys are never slow to tell you that danger is their watchword, that their life is rich in incident – 'one challenge after another', 'never a dull moment', 'no two jobs alike' etc.,etc. Pah! Okay, so it's tough at times, but take it from a seasoned schmovie-goer, the duties of Mr Average Stuntman are, at best, routine.

The expert has a standard repertoire of 'really dangerous things to do'. He has to know how to take a punch on the jaw first of all, and how to throw one: these are the basics. He must know how to fall off a high roof convincingly, drive cars at high speed up ramps, so that they tip over and plunge into a lake. All in all, a stuntman is just a dummy they want to use twice. Someone experienced enough not to die on the first take, in case they need to shoot it again later.

No gang of ruthless outlaws in a Western adventure would dare confront the sheriff in the saloon without first making sure they had with them at least four competent stuntmen: one to be smacked over the head with a bottle; another to be hit squarely across the back with a breakable chair; a third to be knocked sideways over a banister rail on to a carefully-positioned card-table which collapses to break his fall; and one last one to be thrown out of the saloon window into the street. As I say, quite routine, and most of it purely for show. The windows are not made of ordinary glass – it is a special sort that splinters on impact without cutting anyone. The bottles are made of something inoffensive, too, such as toffee or wax. You can tell that they don't hurt, because in some films *real* actors have agreed to be hit on the head with them.

> *Blow-Out* (1981) A prostitute is being molested by her pimp who has been drinking. When he tries to force her back on to the bed, she takes a bottle that is two-thirds full of liquor and clouts him over the head with it. The bottle breaks into little pieces, but there is no sign of the liquor at all.

> *Dirty Harry* (1971) We must assume that the pimp above bought all his drink from the guy in this picture, who seems to be doing a roaring trade selling empty wine bottles to the public. He wraps one of them up for a customer, who takes it and smashes it across the man's neck. The bottle breaks but no wine spills out.

In a fire or explosion, the first person to catch alight will be the stuntman. He usually staggers about with flames leaping all over his back, head down, screaming and screaming, and then either makes for the nearest window and jumps through it, or slips hastily out of shot to be sprayed with foam by attendant firemen before he really gets hurt.

> *The Towering Inferno* (1974) Robert Wagner is trapped inside an office halfway up a burning skyscraper. He does a sensible thing first: wraps wet towels around his head and makes off into the flames to get help. And I reckon he would probably make it, too, if he didn't do a stupid thing immediately afterwards. A couple of yards into the room, he stops for a moment, bends over a table that is on fire, waits until his towels catch light, and then runs screaming through a pane of glass.

When the stuntman drops off a roof or balcony, he always dives out of the bottom of the shot, or behind a conveniently located wall, fence or lorry, because that is where the air-bed has been hidden that he is going to land on. This makes sense: a man who plunges to his death from a tall building has got to land on a mattress of some kind, otherwise the fall would kill him.

On the other hand, if the director wants to go the whole way and show the body hitting the ground, he has two alternatives, both likely to come to grief. First, he can use a dummy, and we know what happens to them. Second, he could use a stuntman. In the latter case, a mattress then has to be concealed at ground level, where the audience can't see it, to break his fall.

> *I, The Jury* (1982) Mike Hammer (Armande Assante) shoots a gangland fugitive out of his hiding place in a tree. The mattress he falls on to has been carefully covered with leaves so that it won't show up onscreen. But the first thing that happens when the man hits it is that all the leaves fly off in every direction until the mattress is in full view to anyone who was looking out for it.

Hidden Extras

> *The Blood Beast Terror* (1967) The most thrilling moment in the whole film comes as a man tiptoes alone across a darkened laboratory at night, followed closely by the shadow of. . .something! A claw, or a pincer,

> cast across the end of a bookcase. What can it be? The tension builds, you sink lower into your seat, waiting for it to grab him by the shoulder. Suddenly. . .you realize what it is. It's the shadow of the microphone trying to catch the sound he is making as he moves around the room.

Everybody has their own favourite aspect of schmovie-going and their own dark areas, too, the ones they are not so keen on. For me, camera shadows and microphones caught in shot make up a tiny corner of the sport that holds only slight interest. But for the sake of completeness, I have succumbed to the 'but you *can't* leave them out. . .' lobby by sneaking a brief mention of them in here.

Microphones pop up in an assortment of places, and in some films, such as *The Last Voyage* (1960), can almost be looked on as another member of the cast. The clearest ones are those reflected in mirrors and other shiny surfaces: a wall-mirror *(The Black Stallion,* 1979; Agatha, 1978); across a car windscreen *(Venom,* 1980); a TV screen *(Absence of Malice,* 1981; *Harlequin,* 1980); or a farmhouse window *(Torn Curtain,* 1966). By far the best example of a mike mis-take happens, surprisingly, in a prestigious Alan Parker film.

> *Midnight Express* (1978) Towards the end of the picture, jailed drug-smuggler Billy Hayes is being led up a pathway inside a Turkish prison by a guard. He cries out 'No! No! No! No!' all the way along, and the only reason you can hear what he is shouting is thanks to the somewhat obvious sound-technician running across the courtyard below him, holding the microphone boom above his head, unaware that he is in shot.

The Schmovie 20

The Schmovie 20

As I write these words, I am on the line to Steven Spielberg in Los Angeles, or rather to his office in Los Angeles, and his chummy personal secretary, Julie. Together we are in the throes of setting up an exclusive interview for The Schmovie Club with this marvellous director, to discover at long last how some of the mis-takes in his films came about.

While I am waiting for the exact date and time, perhaps I should recap on why you need to know so many rules and guidelines in order to become a fully operational schmovie-goer. No, it's not because we don't have enough mis-takes to fill a whole book! And no, before you ask, it's not to pad out the chapters to make up for the fact that we don't know why half the goofs happened in the first place. Although, since you mention it, one of the most disappointing features about kack-spotting as a science, is that very often the reasons behind the mis-takes are almost impossible to come by. If you ask a director about a flaw in one of his pictures, you are inviting blank looks, and long weighty silences. Sometimes he can't remember; sometimes he can, but doesn't want to tell you – so what's the point in asking?

> *The 39 Steps* (1978) Robert Powell plays Richard Hannay, who, in the early scenes, walks around his London flat wearing an expensive floral dressing-gown with a silver quilted collar. Soon after, he travels to Scotland, jumping off the train along the way. He arrives at the home of a Scottish landowner without an ounce of luggage, and has to be given a fresh set of clothes – dinner-suit, shirt, a pair of shoes, and that exact-same dressing-gown he wore at the start of the film! Same floral pattern, same silver quilted collar.

Sure of my facts, I cornered Mr Powell outside a theatre one evening and asked him about what I thought was an absolute cut-and-dried howler of an oversight. 'Oh no, it was a different dressing-gown,' he gushed instantly. 'Definitely not the same one. I remember. Goodbye.' And that was that. Well, I'm sorry, but it looked to *me* like the same one, Robert, and to a number of other people, too. So I shall have to leave you as a Schmovie apprentice in the dark, and let you check it for yourself when you get the chance. But you see, here we have our chief problem. It is all too easy for them to deny the existence of a mis-take. They may be telling the truth, but similarly and quite rightly, they may well be protecting the integrity of the film, and won't want to be thought of as ratting on the wardrobe department or the continuity girl. As the audience, we have no way of knowing what the real truth is, which is why I am on the telephone chasing Mr Spielberg, to ask him if he is prepared to rat on a few of his own pictures.

I have been hanging on now for quite a while at my own expense, but since this is the fifth time I've rung, and since I think I detect a certain reluctance at the other end to specify a rendezvous point, or a day, or *anything,* I am going to stick with it for a little bit longer, and damn the cost. So while I am arranging the finer details of our meeting, such as whether there is going to be one or not, this might be a good moment to give you the final tool you will need in your quest for kack, our last step towards understanding how the various components are assembled and locked together into the finished film.

The Cliché Code sets out a list of what are called the 'Always and Nevers' of film-making – simple truths that apply universally in the making of films, which enschmoviasts call the Schmovie 20 (even though there are, in fact, 25 altogether!).

1. Fire-extinguishers are never used to put out fires

That is a fact in movies, and if they *are* used, it will only be after every conceivable alternative has been tried first. Faced with anything from the tiniest spark to the most raging, out-of-control inferno, no one in the film will tackle it unless all other, more unsuitable methods have failed.

> *San Ferry Ann* (1965) A tent catches light on a campsite, so the first thing the owner does is look for something to combat the flames – and reaches, as you'd expect, for his guitar. After swiping at the tent with that for a few seconds, he tries a tea-towel. While he is flapping away at the flames, another chap comes to help, bringing a fire-extinguisher with him, and carefully and methodically squirts foam all over the tent-owner, making sure none of it goes anywhere near the fire.

> *Exorcist II: The Heretic* (1977) Richard Burton attacks a fire in the basement of a mental-health clinic by running around, striking madly at the flames with, of all things, a crutch. He lunges madly with it, swinging

> and thwacking, until Ellen Burstyn rushes in and has the good sense to take a fire-extinguisher off the nearby wall and put the fire out with that.

There seems to be no end to their ingenuity in this respect. In *Where Eagles Dare* (1969) German soldiers fight a fire in a munitions store by sloshing at it with wet mops; in *Captain Clegg* (1982), not having the benefit of a fully-trained mop squad, a picture-frame is used instead; in *The Phantom of the Opera* (1962) Herbert Lom tries a canvas rubbish-bag; in *Fun With Dick and Jane* (1976), as a gesture, the guests in a restaurant flap napkins at a small fire on their table; in *Krakatoa – East of Java* (1968) it was garden shovels they used, as I recall, while in *Superman II* (1980) I seem to remember a man *kicking* the flames when his car sets on fire. In *The Intelligence Men* (1965) even the chap who says he has come to refill the fire-extinguishers at a Covent Garden theatre is, in fact, carrying a cross-bow in his case – no sign of any refills. Anything will do, it seems, just so long as it is in no way suited for the task.

On the other hand, fire-extinguishers do make excellent weapons. They are a good standby in any tussle, when a director feels he ought to have something fresh and original, a new twist, in preference to the standard arsenal: guns are okay, but somehow so quick and so final; knuckles have their advantages – they're easily portable for a start, but a little tame for the modern audience, and it can take such a long time to knock an adversary out with them. When something heavy and blunt is called for, something that will stun an opponent rather than kill him, then a director will usually opt for a fire-extinguisher.

Richard Widmark almost has his skull broken with a fire-extinguisher in *A Prize of Gold* (1955); Sean Connery knocks an enemy agent over a banister with one in *Diamonds Are Forever* (1971); Roger Moore tries to blind a guard with another in *Moonraker* (1979); Sean Connery, in *Never Say Never Again* (1984), fends off a shark with one; and *Blindfold* (1965) contains the longest sustained attack with a fire-extinguisher ever recorded on film.

But they are not simply used for bodily violence. A fire-extinguisher is just as good for breaking open a locker door *(Rocky,* 1976), smashing a hospital window *(Bullitt,* 1968), and rousing schoolboys from their beds in the middle of the night *(National Lampoon's Animal House,* 1978).

2. Fog always pours out from behind a wall, tree or very large rock.

They call it 'Fun-fog' in the industry, the kind of localized mist, a meteorological freak, that only happens in films. Used strategically, it will mask out modern traffic flowing past in the background of an historical picture, hide where the set ends, or the fact that they have no set at all. If you see fog or mist on a set or location, then seven times out of ten it's hiding something – likely as not the machine making the fog. It has to be hidden somewhere in the picture, so they tuck it away behind a clump of bushes *(Crack in the World,* 1965), a wall *(Knights of the Round Table,* 1953), some trees *(Hawk the Slayer,* 1980), or behind a rocky outcrop *(One Million Years BC,* 1966).

There is nothing like a bit of dense fun-fog to give a sinister period feel to a set. The designers and decorators can only do so much to bestow on a scene the *look* of Victorian London – the Wright's Coal Tar Soap posters, Bovril advertisements, the hansom cabs, damp brick walls, beggars selling matches, cackling strumpets leaning in a doorway, hitching up their skirts – 'Lookin' for a good time, deeery??'; the clip-clop of horses and the clatter of carriage wheels on cobble – but fog gives it real atmosphere. A regular pea-souper is what is required, caused by one stage-hand burning charcoal out of sight behind the set, and another walking round with a can of dry ice puffing it here and there into the corners to ensure an even gloom. Fog evokes a mood that a few backdrops, props and costumes, however well-designed they may be, cannot achieve by themselves.

> *Moss Rose* (1947) contains a flashback to old London Town, where all the fog is emerging from behind a wall at the end of the street, and that is where it stays, too. It doesn't creep into side-alleys, it just stays where it is, where the man with the fog-machine left it.

3. You will always find one man in disaster movies who, in the face of mounting calamity, and shunning all warnings to the contrary, is convinced that there is nothing whatsoever to be alarmed about.

'Now *really* Richard, you don't honestly expect me to believe that, do you?' he'll say, pooh-poohing the very idea of catastrophe, a split-second before the ocean liner he is on capsizes, or a shuddering volcano erupts, or as his airliner spins out of control and plummets into the sea. 'Nonsense, that's impossible. . .' as another 15 floors of that tower-block he designed are blown out of the sky, and as more and more guests tumble from twelfth-storey windows with their tuxedos ablaze. He surveys the devastation, weighs up the loss of life against the prospect of things getting better, then urges, 'Everything is going to be fine. Trust me. . .', and is invariably proved wrong at once.

He is always someone with a vested interest in keeping the status as quo as possible: perhaps he runs a hotel on a mountain threatened by an avalanche and doesn't want to lose his trade because of a few wild scare stories; or he's the mayor of a seaside resort whose holiday business is put in jeopardy by a visiting shark. Look for the vested interest, and you've found your man.

4. It never 'just rains' in movies.
Rain is always torrential, otherwise we wouldn't be able to see it on the screen. Drizzle isn't enough, spits and spots won't show up. So rain always has to gush down windows and drains, swill across roofs and rattle defiantly on carriages and cabs – another climactic oddity peculiar to films, and known as 'Dunwanna rainfall' in the business, after the alleged cry of one thirties' director who shouted to his effects-men, 'Dunwanna shower, dunwanna squawl, gimme a deluge or nothin' at all!'

The weather is generally not out to do anyone any favours. If a deluge is required, they may choose the perfect day to shoot it – the skies are dark, the forecast looks grimmer than ever, and all is going well. But once it starts raining, it won't stay raining. Once they have managed to get a couple of shots in the can, the storm clouds that looked so promising earlier will scatter as the sun works its way through. They will be obliged to carry on in bright sunshine, and when all these shots are spliced together, the ground will be wet, dry, wet, dry alternately (*Halloween*, 1978; *Subterfuge*, 1968).

The answer is to film, whenever possible, in the controlled conditions of the studio, where instant rain is on tap, and comes in two varieties. The first is sprinkler-rain, created by hanging shower-heads at intervals above the set to give the unfortunate effect of localized downpours every couple of feet.

> *The Longest Day* (1962) General Norman Cota of the US 29th Division is inside his army HQ wondering whether inclement weather is about to scupper the D-Day landings. Outside, his hut it is raining very heavily, but from sprinklers – so that it falls in some places and not in others. At the rear of the set is a backdrop photograph of the army barracks and some trees. But they must have been shooting this one scene for a helluva long time, because the photograph is soaking up the wet from the puddles on the ground, and an embarrassing damp patch has begun to creep slowly up the background.

The other sort of rain is made by using a short length of hosepipe, punctured in places to let the water dribble out, and hung over windows, which is why rain always pours, runs, streams down window panes in the movies.

> *Khartoum* (1966) Prime Minister Gladstone (Ralph Richardson) holds a crucial meeting with General Gordon (Charlton Heston) in an office on a railway

station. Outside, rain is pelting against the window – which is puzzling to say the least, because the platform is overhung by a giant canopy, so there is no way that rain, however fierce, could reach the window of the office.

If all else fails, and all else usually does, a director can call on the local fire-brigade to help him out. When business is slow, a half-dozen firemen may turn out to train their hoses on the set, creating an instant thunderstorm. For the price of a pint each and a ploughman's lunch, they'll gladly give the actors a good dousing for most of the morning. However, if you're prepared to go one step further and slip a few quid into the 'widows and orphans', then a steady torrent could well set in for the rest of the day. The problem with hosed rain is that it tends to fall in a straight line – wherever the man with the nozzle happens to be pointing it at the time (*Heaven's Above,* 1963; *The Phantom of the Opera,* 1962).

Another great idea is to film the scene without any rain at all and then superimpose a shower on to the picture afterwards.

Mysterious Island (1961) A hot-air balloon soars up into the sky during a heavy rainstorm. And yet, even when the balloon is floating above the clouds, it is still pouring with rain.

Or, of course, they could just stick with real rain on location, and hope that it keeps up for the whole time they need it.

Close Encounters of the Third Kind (1977) At the point where Richard Dreyfuss has become so obsessed with the image of Devil's Tower that he's built himself a scale-model of it in his living-room, it is raining very heavily outside the French windows. In despair, he wanders over to look out into the garden, by which time the rain has stopped and his neighbours are out spraying their cars and playing baseball.

Which reminds me – Steven Spielberg. I'm told that he is out of town until next week; that he might not want to be quoted in a book of this sort anyway, and that Julie is unsure of her schedule for the rest of the morning, and will call me back. Good, now we're getting somewhere.

5. Whenever plain-clothes detectives tail a suspect, they always do it in the most obvious way.

Stealth is unheard of! The chase begins quite often in the lobby of the suspect's hotel. One of the cops will be sitting slumped in an armchair behind a copy of the *Chicago Herald,* sometimes with two peepy-holes

cut out for him to peer through. Once in the street, a second cop will tag along and the pair of them will keep within feet of their quarry, behaving so obtrusively that they couldn't help *but* be noticed. If the suspect stops to buy a hotdog or kick a football back to some kids playing in the street (as he usually will), the detectives stop too, throwing themselves into some spur-of-the-moment window-shopping, or ducking behind a pillar with just the brim of their hats showing.

Ideally, both should be wearing the internationally accepted 'Me-Follow-You' gear – white raincoat with the collar pulled up about the ears, broad baggy trousers with broad turn-ups that resemble ankle-pelmets, and the compulsory trilby hat.

When the suspect returns to his apartment, the pursuers wait outside. They know that if they were to take up a surveillance position on a rooftop some blocks away and watch his movements through binoculars, then the sun would only catch on the lenses and give the game away – they've seen it happen in too many other films to fall for that one. So they keep watch on his apartment block by hanging about under the suspect's window at night, lolling against railings, lighting cigarettes in the direct beam of a street-lamp and waiting for him to come out. Usually, so much lolling and smoking goes on while they are waiting, that the suspect is given ample time to slip out of the back of the building completely unnoticed.

6. 'A car-chase ensues'.

These four words in a script are enough to send any director scurrying to his copy of the Code to find out what he should do next.

A car-chase performs two functions: it pads out a weak story, and creates the maximum amount of spectacle, noise and mess at the very least cost. But the truth is that audiences have had it up to here with car-chases. It is no longer enough for two black Jaguars to zig-zag across the road, brakes squealing, tyres belching smoke, and skid around a few corners with their headlamps on. We set a higher price on our attention than that. We have come to expect a precise sequence of stunts and therefore *car-chases always contain most, if not all, of the following:*

1. One car must run into a stack of cartons, crates or baskets, and swerve into five or six dustbins. Anything like this is cheap, makes a terrible din and looks impressive on the screen in short doses.

2. You also feel seriously shortchanged if one car doesn't dive through the fruit and vegetable display outside a greengrocer's shop, tearing down the canopy and spilling oranges into the road.

3. Another car should run up a concealed ramp on two wheels and overturn, possibly careering into the wall of a garage, or through the side of a parked container truck, or even belly-flopping on top of a crowd of other cars.

4. A fourth car will break through a police-barrier or a 'Danger – Road Closed' sign.

5. One should fly off the road and hit a tree, or dive into a lake and explode.

6. Yet another must smash headlong through the plate-glass window of a prestige car-showroom or a department store and explode.

7. And a final car should soar off a cliff-edge, drift silently downwards with its bonnet and boot flapping, hit the bottom of a quarry and explode.

It is also fairly customary for one car to pull up alongside another as they drive, to try and nudge it over the edge of a cliff, but the one that does the nudging is always the one that ends up in the quarry. In older films it is quite easy to tell which car will eventually be destroyed – because it is always the cheapest: the one they rescued from a scrap-yard, to be given a quick lick of paint and put back on the road just for the chase sequence.

Three additional points: a) Drivers only find that their brakes have been tampered with when they are steering along the most perilous mountain pass with a sheer drop to one side; b) If the chase is set anywhere in Paris or Italy, at least one of the cars will be driven down three flights of stone steps; c) If the police are involved, and doing part of the chasing, then they will almost certainly lose 90 per cent of their vehicles in the process, and go on to damage the rest when they use them as a road-block in the hope of bringing the villain's car to a halt. To my knowledge, this ruse has never worked to this day, because most gangs of villains have great foresight and employ trained stuntmen to drive their getaway vehicles: someone who can run it up a ramp and over the top of the police cars, or straight through any barricade and out at the other side.

7. When an ocean liner starts to sink, there is always one man on board who dons his wife's best frock and headscarf and smuggles himself into the women-and-children-only lifeboat.

This became so regular a ploy at one time that ship's officers began changing their regular abandon-ship call to 'Women, men-dressed-as-women, and children first. . .' The immediate problem facing this guy is that so many other people have to be crammed into the lifeboat beside himself, people far more important to the storyline than he is. One average-sized boat has to accommodate the lead actors who are going to survive the disaster; a handful of readily-deadlies taken along to drop into the water and drown when the boat becomes too full and breaks from the winch; a despairing hag bawling 'My baby! My baby!'; some non-frolicking extras to scream and cry and comfort each other during and after the disaster, and maybe even a dummy or two. No room for the man in a frock at all.

If clichés could be graded and awarded points for most frequent and hackneyed usage, this man would come second only to the prisoner who escapes from a POW camp dressed as a washerwoman.

8. People always turn on their radio to hear a newsflash that directly concerns them.

'We interrupt this broadcast to bring you the latest news on the dangerous convict, Johnnie the Jinx, who escaped last night from Wimborough Top Security Prison. He is thought to be armed, extremely dangerous and hiding somewhere in the Wimborough area. Police advise residents to stay in their homes and lock their doors. We now return you to Vic Nasicorne and His Up-Tempo Catapult Seven. . .' You can bet that anyone who turns on their radio and hears something of this nature, will switch it off and straight away hear a knock at the door. Whoever or whatever has escaped and is on the loose, will walk in, tie everyone up and hold them hostage for the rest of the picture.

9. Citizens in sci-fi films always follow a set procedure when dealing with monsters on the loose, or with visitors from other planets.

Having first left the creature to savage a few non-frolickers from the bottom of the cast-list as a sample of how dangerous he is, the characters in the film stick to a strict order for tackling the menace. First, the ordinary citizens attack it – a useless move that simply has to fail; if it didn't, the film would be over in less than 10 minutes. Then the citizens call in the police, and the police attack it, and fail for much the same reason, but only after a specialized team of gonners has been sent in to kill it, all of whom are killed themselves within a few seconds. So the police call in an expert. He reckons that the creature is a reasoning and reasonable being, capable of compassion and kindness, and so the expert tries to bargain with it, which is usually the turning-point of the film, because the creature will then attack the expert and perhaps capture his busty daughter, and cause the expert to lose all sense of logic. He will call in the military at once and tell *them* to attack it. When they fail, too, they call in another expert who, on the spur of the moment, will dream up some fantastic plan to deal with the emergency, and the plan will be to set a trap for the creature. The trap always works, simply because the film is almost at an end and the money's running out. The creature is destroyed, the expert's busty daughter is released, and everyone in the cast goes home smiling, forgetting it ever happened.

10. There's always a token sailor in every two-bit sleazy dive.
For as long as I can remember, schmovie-goers have always shown an intense interest in sailors on shore-leave.

To the director's keen eye, nothing adds that sense of run-down tackiness to a night-club, dance-hall or bar than a sailor placed prominently in shot. Any dingy, smoky club or theatre that is full of harlots, gamblers, pimps and drunks will also have in it somewhere a sailor, flopped unconscious over a table, dancing cheek-to-cheek in a corner, or pressed close to the footlights, beating his hand on the stage.

11. Skulls always face the camera.
This is self-explanatory. A director will want to drain every last drop of suspense he can out of a horror scene, and skulls are, quite frankly, not the least bit scary if you see them from the back. So whether it is standing on a shelf at the back of the professor's study or slung carelessly on the ground, a skull will always face the camera.

12. Indians always have their own music.
A privilege accorded to few other characters in films – Dracula, the Cavalry, Princess Leia and the Pink Panther being the main ones. Indian music rarely varies too far from the low-key bom-bom-bom-bom-diddle-bom-bom tune that is always played when the Cherokees first trot through the gulch on their way to burn down a ranch and to massacre Martha, little Billy and Kip Carlton's men. The rule here relates mostly to the volume of the music on the soundtrack. If you can only hear the Indians banging their drums, or see their smoke-signals, then you will be treated to nothing more than bom-bom-bom-bom-diddle-bom-bom. But if you get to see them, and a BLAAAAAAA!-Man points and shouts 'Injuns!' then it will be a cacophonous BOMM-BOMM-BOMM-BOMM-DIDDLE-BOMM-BOMM!

13. Any room with deep religious significance is always flooded in sunlight and jammed to the ceiling with Holy Bibles, crucifixes, paintings of archangels startling sheep, and cheap pot figurines of the Virgin Mary in a variety of text-book poses.

The Virgin Mary watching over Gentle Jesus, the Virgin Mary cuddling Gentle Jesus, the Virgin Mary inspecting Gentle Jesus to see if his clothes need swaddling or not: in other words, all the clues you must have in order to be able to say with unbridled confidence that 'religion goes on in here, I'm sure of it!' Film-makers adopt the same policy as they do for stock scientists, that it is not enough for a man simply to tell the audience that he is holy, you won't believe him until he proves it with icons, idols, trinkets and a thousand other giveaway clues to his faith.

14. Small circuses and fairs are always in dire financial trouble.
The boss is heading for ruin, he needs a big draw to pull in the crowds, creditors are flapping final demands at him, and his business is about to be swallowed up by a larger, more prosperous concern across town. Further, circus people never let a film go by without mentioning that they have sawdust in their veins, or without singing a song that rhymes clowns with ups-and-downs and merry-go-rounds.

15. Impregnable fortresses never are.
Listen out for anyone in an adventure movie who says that a daunting mountain stronghold is impregnable, a hilltop keep inaccessible or a missile-base indestructible. These follow the same lines as ships that are unsinkable, plans that are foolproof and prison camps from which there is no escape, and all prove to be completely the opposite before the closing credits, otherwise there would be no film. Any crack team can break into an impregnable fortress. They simply approach it from the direction that everyone inside has dismissed as not worth worrying about; they breach the walls, distract the patrolling guards by throwing a handful of gravel or a small rock into the opposite corner of the courtyard, and then choke them from behind with cheese-wires. After that, the explosives can be primed, any prisoners released, secret devices, weapons or plans grabbed and pocketed, and an escape route sorted out – and it happens with a regularity that is statistically laughable.

16. Angry conductors in films always snap their batons.

17. Anyone killed in a landslide or under fallen masonry always dies with one hand sticking out as the dust clears.

18. Men with crippling financial or family problems always stop shaving until their luck changes.

19. Spaceships in films made before 1968 are always exclamation-mark shaped, and have fins and portholes.
In films made after *2001: A Space Odyssey* (1968), all space-craft are approximately a quarter of a million times bigger than they need to be to carry out the tasks for which they were built.

20. Anyone who drops from a great height and falls on to his back, always lies with one of his legs cocked.

If he falls face-down instead, then he will lie with one of his arms cocked.

21. It doesn't matter whereabouts on his body a man gets hit, blood always trickles out of the corner of his mouth.

22. The good guys in horror movies say, 'In God's name coachman, ride like the wind!' while the bad guys always say, 'Ride like the Devil!'

23. Drunken Mexican bandits in a saloon always pull out their revolvers and shoot the glass from the mirror, the paintings off the wall, and the liquor bottles from the shelf behind the bar.

24. In spy films, anyone rifling through a drawer and photographing secret documents always hears someone coming, and has ample time to tidy everything away and hide before the door opens and the light is switched on.

It is the custom that good guys wait behind the door with the butt of their revolver raised, ready to club the visitor, while bad guys run behind the curtains and stand quietly with their shoes showing, hoping they won't be noticed.

25. The villains in big-budget spy movies always make every conceivable effort to trap and capture the hero, and when they have him where they want him, refuse to kill him.

Rather, they give him a tour of their underground missile complex or their rocket launch-pad, pointing out features of interest, taunting and goading him until he has had sufficient opportunity to work out a means of escape. The point here is that would-be world dominators *would be* world dominators if they didn't spend so much time explaining their plans to the person most likely to foil them.

People often stop me and ask, 'You mean these things happen in every single film, regardless of who made it or when it was released?' To which I usually reply, 'I wish you hadn't asked me that!' Because no, they don't always happen – I lied. No theory is so watertight that it is without exceptions. In *Wolfen* (1981), *Jaws* (1975), *The Fog* (1979) and *Mara Maru* (1952) fires are put out using fire-extinguishers. And in *Ulzana's Raid* (1972) the Indians don't have their own music, although the little boy in the film *is* called Billy.

There are bound to be a few renegades who break free from the pack and ignore the Cliché Code. The best that can be said of The Schmovie 20 is that they are all universally true, except for when they don't apply.

Flash! Bang! Codswallop! What a Picture!

Flash! Bang! Codswallop! What a Picture!

And that's it! We have come to the end of the lollipop as far as your schmovie-training is concerned. You should now be a fully-equipped enschmoviast – a kack-spotting machine, able to take your rightful place in seat E23 at any cinema, to apply the rules laid down in this book and spoil the film for everyone sitting around you.

Doubtless, along the way, I have offended many existing schmovie-buffs, who find that their favourite mis-take has not been included anywhere in these pages, but that's the way the cliché crumbles, I'm afraid. There are so many mis-takes around, I couldn't possibly have included them all. And even though the book is finished, the quest for kack goes on. New members are joining the Schmovie Club every week, as our organization around the world goes from strength to strength. Too many goofs remain undiscovered, too many mysteries unsolved, for us to abandon the quest now.

The following are just a few of the more baffling examples that have been disinterred of late. If you can explain any of them, or any of the other mis-takes dotted throughout the book, do write and let us know.

The Smallest Show on Earth (1957) A young married couple inherit a tiny cinema in Sloughborough, a town in the north of England. Yet when they arrive in the town for the first time to inspect their property, they climb out of the taxi in front of Hammersmith underground station in London.

Voyage of the Damned (1976) At the part of the film that is set outside the German Army HQ in Hamburg, 1939, a bright red London bus appears to travel past the end of the drive behind a parked lorry.

Mouse on the Moon (1963) Terry-bloody-Thomas takes a snapshot of David Kossoff, who is holding an armful of shower-heads that are going to be used as stabilizers on his space-rocket. But when the picture is developed in London later on, the stabilizers are not in Kossoff's arms but attached to the rocket itself.

The Deadly Mantis (1957) Experts go in search of a military aircraft that has been attacked by the Mantis and has crash-landed at the North Pole. They find the fuselage with a huge hole ripped out of the side and snow pouring through into the cockpit. The only sounds you can hear are the wind howling and a steady sshhhpppp-ssshhhppp-ssshhhppppp noise. You assume that this is the sound of the damaged instruments malfunctioning, and it takes you a little while before you realize that the sshhhpppp-ssshhhppp-ssshhhhpppppp-ing corresponds directly with the clouds of snow coming through the hole, and then a little while longer before it dawns on you that the reason the snow is coming through the hole at all is because there is a man standing outside with a broom, sweeping snowflakes into the plane, making the sshhhppp-ssshhhppp-ssshhhpppppp-ing sound as he brushes.

Airport '80 – The Concorde (1979) In order to fire an emergency flare, George Kennedy opens the cockpit window of Concorde while it is in flight and sticks his hand out: an act of idiocy which, I am informed, would not only take his hand clean off, but would suck the entire crew out of the window after it.

Assault on Precinct 13 (1976) Why was the film called this, when all the action seems to take place on Precinct 9?

A Run for Your Money (1949) Why does a shopkeeper who has just been raided by a mob call the police by running into the street and shouting, '9-9-9!'?

The Greatest Show on Earth (1957) Why does the cinema janitor run in to announce that the cat has had six kittens: 'Four girls and one boy'?

On top of these, we have a clutch of mysterious strangers from various movies, whom we have never been able to explain away satisfactorily.

The Great Escape (1963) When Steve McQueen is riding his motorbike towards the Swiss Border at the end of the film, who is the little man running along the side of a fence to his right, trying to duck out of sight, only to slip and fall over, attracting more attention to himself than ever?

Bullitt (1968) Who is the man standing outside Safeway's supermarket in San Francisco, waving his arms like crazy, and pointing out to the drivers in the car-chase which way they should go?

The Brigand of Kandahar (1965) Who is the man in the grey cloak in an Indian village being interviewed by British soldiers, who appears in the film two or three times without his presence ever being explained?

Circus World (1964) When the big top goes up in flames at the end, who is the man in the black cape, watching the catastrophe at close quarters, giggling and clapping his hands as the tent billows out and collapses around him?

The final mystery is: how is it that the deputy sheriff in *Captain Apache* (1971) is shot with a knife? The only theory anyone has put forward to date is that the guy walks out of his office, is ambushed in the street by two men, one of whom has a knife and stabs him with it. In defence, he shoots at them twice, then struggles back into the office – with the knife in his chest. Could be the case, but we can't be absolutely sure. See it for yourself and make up your mind.

And that really *is* it! I wish you luck in your quest, and hope that you derive as much personal satisfaction from being an out-and-out killjoy as the rest of us do. I can only repeat the pleas I set out earlier in the book: go to your task with humour and humility. Be as kind as you can, and make as many allowances for artistic licence as possible . . . *then* pull the film to pieces.

Oh, and Steven Spielberg. . .I've left the phone off the hook, Steve, so you can forget it now, okay?